From Laura
Aug. 2004

ATHENA SINGS:
WAGNER AND THE GREEKS

Richard Wagner's knowledge of and passion for Greek drama was so profound that for Friedrich Nietzsche, Wagner was Aeschylus come alive again. Surprisingly little has been written about the pervasive influence of classical Greece on the quintessentially German master. In this elegant and masterfully argued book, renowned opera critic Father Owen Lee describes for the contemporary reader what it might have been like to witness a dramatic performance of Aeschylus in the theatre of Dionysus in Athens in the fifth century B.C. – something that Wagner himself undertook to do on several occasions, imagining a performance of *The Oresteia* in his mind, reading it aloud to his friends, providing his own commentary, and relating the Greek classic drama to his own romantic view.

Father Lee also uses Wagner's writings on Greece and entries from his wife's diaries to cast new light on *Tristan und Isolde, Die Meistersinger, Parsifal,* and especially the mighty *Ring* cycle, where Wagner made extensive use of Greek elements to give structural unity and dramatic credibility to his Nordic and Germanic myths. No opera fan, argues Father Lee, can really understand Wagner saving Brünhilde without knowing the Athena who, in Greek drama, first brought justice to Athens.

Written with a clarity and depth of knowledge that have characterized all Father Lee's books on the classics of Greece and Rome and made his six other volumes on opera bestsellers, *Athena Sings* traces the profound influence – an influence few music lovers are aware of – that Greek theatre and culture had on the most German of composers and his revolutionary musical dramas.

FATHER M. OWEN LEE, CSB, is a Catholic priest and professor emeritus of Classics at St Michael's College, University of Toronto. He has been a commentator for the Texaco Metropolitan Opera radio broadcasts for many years, and is the author of a number of books on opera, including *A Season of Opera: From Orpheus to Ariadne* (UTP 1998) and *Wagner: The Terrible Man and His Truthful Art* (UTP 1999).

ATHENA SINGS

Wagner and the Greeks

M. OWEN LEE

UNIVERSITY OF TORONTO PRESS
Toronto Buffalo London

© University of Toronto Press Incorporated 2003
Toronto Buffalo London
Printed in Canada

ISBN 0-8020-8795-7 (cloth)
ISBN 0-8020-8580-6 (paper)

Printed on acid-free paper

National Library of Canada Cataloguing in Publication

Lee, M. Owen, 1930–
Athena sings : Wagner and the Greeks / M. Owen Lee.

Includes bibliographical references and index.
ISBN 0-8020-8795-7 (bound).   ISBN 0-8020-8580-6 (pbk.)

1. Wagner, Richard, 1813–1883 – Criticism and interpretation.
2. Wagner, Richard, 1813–1883 – Knowledge – Greek drama.
I. Title

ML410.W13L48 2003   782.1′092   C2003-902153-X

University of Toronto Press acknowledges the financial assistance to
its publishing program of the Canada Council for the Arts and the
Ontario Arts Council.

University of Toronto Press acknowledges the financial support for its
publishing activities of the Government of Canada through the Book
Publishing Industry Development Program (BPIDP).

for
Emmet Robbins

CONTENTS

Preface

ix

ONE

Athena Sings

3

TWO

Intermission

45

THREE

Brünnhilde Sings

53

Notes

89

Bibliography

103

Index

107

PREFACE

This volume expands a lecture I first gave to the Toronto Wagner Society in 1984 and subsequently to the Alumni of St Michael's College in Toronto and to the Wagner Society of Southern California. Its subject, the influence of ancient Greece on the work of Richard Wagner, is one which, despite its importance, was long neglected in Wagner studies outside of Germany. In 1976 the classicist Hugh Lloyd-Jones could find only a single treatment of the theme in English, a pioneering but 'not wholly adequate' 1919 Columbia University dissertation by Pearl C. Wilson. And he searched in vain through the many volumes on Wagner by Ernest Newman for any indication that the most influential English authority on Wagner regarded the subject as of any importance at all.

Several treatments in English on Wagner and the Greeks have since then made their way into print. This is, I believe, the first that attempts to reach an audience that knows more about Wagner than it does about the Greeks. In my first chapter, I try to convey to the Greekless reader what it might have been like to witness a performance of Aeschylus in Athens in the fifth century BC. It was something Wagner himself undertook to do on several occasions, imagining a performance of the *Oresteia* in his mind, or reading its three parts to friends and providing his own commentary. I have chosen, like Wagner, to traverse the *Oresteia* and refer forward to the *Ring*. Michael Ewans, in a volume more scholarly than this one, traverses the *Ring* and refers back to the *Oresteia*. Any reader of this book who wants to go more deeply into these matters will certainly find Ewans illuminating from that reverse perspective.

Perhaps I should apologize to the scholarly for relegating scholarly interests to the endnotes. I thought it best to keep the text conversational, as the lecture was. (That is not to say that the notes lack the lightness of the text.) The translations from Wagner's prose works are my own, and, as the original texts are notoriously frenzied and foggy, I feel obliged to say here that in translating the perfervid passages I have made a determined but I hope not drastic attempt to render them in intelligible English. (Bryan Magee has written, rightly, that Wagner's stylistic faults in writing the prose works were 'compounded' in what is still the only complete English translation of them – that of Ashton Ellis, issued in 1892–9.)

I should like to thank the University of Chicago Press for permission to use the Richmond Lattimore translation of the *Oresteia*, and John St James and the staff of the University of Toronto Press, who have helped me with this as with four previous volumes. Thanks too, for help given in various ways, to Father Doug Hilmer, Ross S. Kilpatrick, Duane W. Roller, and the always encouraging Irene Sloan.

ATHENA SINGS:
WAGNER AND THE GREEKS

CHAPTER ONE

Athena Sings

I

There was a time when Richard Wagner wrote no music for almost six years. He was thirty-six, and had completed three of his ten major operas. *The Flying Dutchman* and *Tannhäuser* had been launched, with varying degrees of success, in Dresden, but *Lohengrin* had not yet found its way to any stage. There was a price on Wagner's head. He had been involved in the 1849 Dresden uprising – providing places for secret meetings, supplying grenades, reporting on troop movements from the tower of the Kreuzkirche, watching the opera house where he was employed go up in smoke. When the uprising failed, he was charged with treason and forced to flee from Germany. Some of his associates were caught and sentenced to death, though the sentences were eventually commuted to long prison terms. Wagner, with forged papers and an assumed name, took up temporary residence in Switzerland. There, beset as he was by political, personal, and financial difficulties, he found he had come to an artistic impasse.

He could write no music. Instead, as the four operas of his *Ring* cycle gradually took shape in his head, he turned out volume upon volume of rabid, fevered, tortured prose. Much of it was political, and all of it touched on the nature of art. Partly to convince others but largely to convince himself, he fashioned an artistic creed so comprehensive and demanding that, when he turned to write music again, that music – the opening pages of the *Ring* – was like nothing he or anyone else had written before.

Wagner later described his state of mind while he wrote the prose works as 'abnormal.'[1] The ideas that fed his imagination in exile were for the most part second-hand and sometimes only half-understood. But eventually they came together with such explosive force that he started composing again, with new vigour and a new aesthetic. And I don't think I exaggerate when I say that the single most important influence on him at the time was Greece – classic Greece of the fifth century BC. Later, Feuerbach, Schopenhauer, and the teachings of Buddhism where to exert comparable and perhaps more pervasive influences on him. But at the time when his whole concept of the theatre was changing, the formative influence was Greece. Witness this passage from the first of his revolutionary prose works, *Art and Revolution*, written in 1849:

One can hardly begin a serious study of our contemporary art without being reminded, at the start, how dependent it is on the art of the Greeks. In fact, our modern art is only one link in the chain of Europe's artistic development, and the beginning was with the Greeks.

Once the Greek spirit had triumphed over the primitive nature-worship of its Asiatic birthplace and set man – beautiful, strong, and free – in the centre of its consciousness, art and politics began to flower. The Greek spirit found its ideal expression in Apollo, the national deity of the Greek peoples. Apollo, who had slain the Python, the dragon of Chaos, who with his lethal weapons had destroyed the proud sons of Niobe, who through his oracle at Delphi had taught those who came seeking responses what it was to be a Greek – and so held the mirror up to man – this Apollo fulfilled the will of Zeus on the earth of Greece. He *was* the Greek people.

We must not think of this Apollo of the springtime of Greece as a delicate youth, dancing with the Muses. Only the later, more sensual art of sculpture represented him thus. No, the great tragic writer Aeschylus saw Apollo as serene and serious and strong. That was also the way the Spartan saw him, when he had developed his body by dancing and wrestling, when as a boy he was taken from his family and packed off on horseback to vigorous training in lands afar, when as young man he advanced in the lists of his comrades through nothing more than his beauty and gentility – the only might and riches he had in his possession. And that was the way the Athenian saw him, too, when all the instincts of his agile body and restless soul drove him to express himself ideally in art, when his voice joined the other voices, full and thund'rous, to sing in chorus the myths of his god, when in the theatre he re-enacted those myths, dancing in strong and graceful movements.

And then in Athens, among their harmonious and well-ordered columns, they massed the broad semicircles of an amphitheatre row on row, and designed the ingenious arrangements of a stage. And at last, to all those other arts, in spontaneous and natural response to an inner urge, the tragic author added words – bold, encompassing words – and so brought *all* the arts into play, and produced that highest conceivable art form, the drama.[2]

That is more than a little rose-tinted, but the enthusiasm in it is infectious, and the ideas – that drama originated in Greece in a religious context, prompted by a natural impulse, and brought together the separate arts of music, dance, architecture, and poetry to serve a single exalted end – were ideas that influenced all of Wagner's subsequent work.

No people before the Greeks had drama as we know it, and the subject of Greek drama was myth – the myths of the people who created drama, performed it, and came to watch it. Wagner continues, ecstatically:

> In the theatre the myths were acted out, clearly and with a sense of awe. Through Apollo there was communicated in the theatre something of the rhythms and music of eternity, something of universal motion and universal being. Everything vital and compelling in the myths, and everything that corresponded in the spectators, was realized in the theatre. Heart and soul, eye and ear, saw and heard and understood the myths.

Nothing seems to have excited Wagner so much about Greek drama as this business of acting out myths that previously had only been imagined and spoken. He was convinced that something of the god Apollo was powerfully unleashed when the myths were represented in the theatre. And he was thrilled that the playwrights wrote their own music, and devised their own staging, and sometimes appeared as actors or chorus leaders in their own works:

The days on which tragedy was performed in Greece were religious occasions. On them the god spoke out clearly and distinctly. And the tragic playwright himself was standing – physically present – in the midst of the measures of the dance, raising the voices of the chorus and revealing in ringing words the utterances of divine wisdom. This was the supreme art form produced by Greece. It was Apollo embodied in real, living art. It was the Greek people at its highest point of truth and beauty.

If the ultimate purpose of theatre was religious, and its themes were mythic so as to reach the spectators at a deep psychological level, then theatre could, Wagner thought, be a powerful means of building up a nation's consciousness. The young Wagner was absorbed in the idea of a united states of Germany, much as, on the other side of the Alps, Verdi – with a wholly different aesthetic – was fired with hopes for the unification of his country. And Wagner hoped for a new Germany whose politics would be nurtured by art, a Germany like the Greece of his imagining – and especially like Athens, with its endless confrontations with its rivals Corinth, Sparta, and Thebes:

Each Greek city was in constant contact with the other, in alliances that shifted daily, in wars that daily took on new shapes, today in success, tomorrow in failure, today oppressed by utmost danger, tomorrow pressing their foe to the point of annihilation, caught up within and without in unceasing activity. In Athens the people streamed together from the state assembly, from the law courts,

from the land, from the ships, from the war, from the far-
thest places, and filled the amphitheatre thirty thousand
strong, to see performed the most profound of all tragedies, the *Prometheus*, to assemble before this powerful
work of art, to see in it themselves, to understand their
own actions, to fuse themselves in inmost union with
their own persons, with their city, with their god – and so
begin again, after profound meditation, the lives which a
few hours before they had spent in unremitting activity ...

Wagner saw the experience of theatre as a kind of religious activity that spoke to an un- or sub-conscious:

The Greek was hushed as the chorus began to sing, and
surrendered as the various elements of the drama conspired together. He listened willingly as the great utterances of fate were revealed to him by the tragic
playwright through the mouths of the gods and heroes on
the stage. In tragedy, the Greek found himself again. He
found his nature's noblest part united with the noblest
part of his entire city assembled. Through the tragic masterpiece there spoke within him, to his inner consciousness, Apollo's oracle. He was man in communication
with his god – he in the universe, the universe in him.

That is how the thirty-six year old Wagner wrote about
the Greek theatre. There are things both factual and
interpretative to disagree with in it – from the emphasis
on the god Apollo rather than the god Dionysus to the
number of thousands who could fit into a Greek theatre
to the unlikely 'hushed' religious awe in which the spec-

tators were held. But for all its inaccuracies the tone of it is remarkable for its time. This is not scholarly German *Altertumswissenschaft* speaking, or the earlier classicism of Goethe, Lessing, Hölderlin, and Winckelmann that sought a return to Greece.[3] Neither is it the dilettante picture of an effete, passionless Greece that was popular in Wagner's day. This strikes a note, in its romantic enthusiasm, in its insistence that Greek art should not be reverted to but reborn, that is not sounded in German comments on Greece till Nietzsche – and of course it was excited talk like this, so different from what anyone heard in the lecture halls of Europe's universities, that drew the promising young classicist to Wagner twenty years later.

We will return to Wagner's prose writings in time, but now I would like, with the aid of some modern criticism, to think and feel us, author and reader, back to a performance in Athens some twenty-five centuries ago, to see what it was that made Wagner so enthusiastic, and propelled him into a new kind of opera. What was the Greek theatre like?

II

We will imagine ourselves at a performance, not of *Prometheus* because we haven't the whole of that trilogy, but of the only trilogy surviving from classic Greece, the *Oresteia* of Aeschylus. Three related plays – *Agamemnon*, *The Libation Bearers*, and *The Eumenides*. They draw on a vast cycle of old myths – Trojan War myths which you, as an Athenian, already know very well. You've seen them dramatized several times already, by other playwrights. In fact you have known these myths since you were a child and read them in Homer. You are coming to the theatre this morning to see and hear how Aeschylus will interpret them with new insight, with words and music and patterned imagery, with spectacular staging – and perhaps with a new ending that will touch you deeply and make you proud to be an Athenian.

So what is this old, familiar story that lies behind our three plays?

Long before Athens came to greatness, in the Greece halfway between myth and history, two brothers – Agamemnon, king of the golden city of Mycenae, and Menelaus, king of the then luxuriant city of Sparta – made a terrible mistake: they married two sisters. Agamemnon married Clytemnestra, an ambitious and determined lady, and Menelaus married Helen, the most beautiful woman in the world.

Meanwhile, across the sea, there lay the rich and powerful kingdom of Troy. A prince of Troy, Paris, came to Sparta on a royal mission, fell in love with Helen, and stole away with her: Helen of Sparta crossed the sea with Paris and became Helen of Troy.

The disgraced Menelaus appealed to his older brother Agamemnon, and Agamemnon gathered all the warrior kings of Greece to undertake a punitive expedition against the rich Asiatic city: united, they would rescue Helen – and they would fill their treasuries, too, with the spoils of Troy.

But the Greek armada, a thousand ships assembled at Aulis, was delayed for weeks by adverse winds. Agamemnon asked his priest why the gods were against him, and was told that a human sacrifice was necessary: he must slay, on the altar of the virgin goddess Artemis, his virgin daughter, his first born – Iphigeneia. The girl was sent for, Agamemnon wielded the sacrificial knife, and the armada got its fair wind.

So the Greeks sailed to Troy – and when they got there, they found the city virtually impregnable within its great walls. They spent ten years fighting the Trojans on the vast field that sloped from the walls down to the sea. The fiercest warrior among the Greeks, Achilles, and the noblest of the Trojans, Hector, and the guilty lover, Paris, were all slain. And finally, by means of the Trojan Horse (a story too familiar to tell here) Agamemnon and his Greeks got inside the walls, and the city fell. The destruction was terrible. But, as Chesterton says, Homer caught up the name of Troy in poetry so wonderful that the name has lived forever after. I travelled to Troy one summer, to stand on the ruins of the wall and look down upon the plain below, where Hector died at the hands of Achilles. For this classicist, it was like a dream.

So Menelaus got his wife Helen back. Somehow they came to terms with her guilt and his barbarism, crossed the sea again to Sparta, and lived happily ever after.

But it did not go so well with Agamemnon. He took, as his part of the spoil, the mad, prophetic princess of Troy, Cassandra – and only one of his ships, his own, came safely back through the storms which punished the cruel Greeks on the return voyage. And when Agamemnon finally reached his own shore, there was a curse on his house awaiting him: in past ages, his ancestors had committed terrible crimes within their own family, and he himself had, rightly or wrongly, slain his eldest daughter.

Who are the people waiting for Agamemnon to return to his palace? First, his wife, Clytemnestra, determined to kill him because he had killed their daughter. As part of her revenge she has taken a lover – Agamemnon's cousin and sworn enemy, Aegisthus. A coward, but a dangerous one. Also waiting is Agamemnon's other daughter, Electra, loyal to him and so virtually enslaved by her mother in the palace. And finally, sent to a king-dom far away so he will not cause any trouble, there is Agamemnon's young son, Orestes. It is for Orestes that the whole trilogy, the *Oresteia*, is named. And it is on his young shoulders that the whole cumulative guilt of the family eventually descends.

Aeschylus picks up the story at that point and contin-ues it in his three related dramas.

Before Wagner fled Germany, when he was still in Dres-den at work on *Lohengrin*, he read Aeschylus's trilogy through for the first time, translated and commented on by Johann Gustav Droysen. He was mightily impressed, and wrote in his autobiography, *Mein Leben*, that all his ideas about what the drama signified, and what the theatre could be, took definite shape under the impact of those impressions.[4] In later life, in the company of friends and admirers, he used to conjure up in his imagi-nation a performance of a Greek drama at the outdoor theatre of Dionysus in the fifth century BC. He would read the text and act it out, interpreting as he went along.

May I invite you, similarly, to feel yourself back some twenty-five centuries, to 458 BC, to Athens on a morning in March? You're an adult male citizen,[5] one of a generation of Athenians who fought off the invading Persians. You're proud of that. Your city, not a large city at the time, defeated the great army of Darius pretty well single-handedly, at Marathon, and ten years later, when the Persians returned under Xerxes, you fought off an even greater army and navy, at Salamis. You had some help with that, from other Greek cities, but you and your fellow Athenians rightly regard yourselves as the saviors of all Greece.

With your father and brothers and sons you turn out of bed early this morning and, unshaven and unbreakfasted (you wear a beard and can snack on something when you get there), you make your way to the theatre in the dark, almost as Catholics go to early Mass on a holy day of obligation. For this is the octave of the feast of the god Dionysus, the god of drama, and every adult male citizen is expected to attend the ceremonies in his honour.

Part of those ceremonies will be seventeen plays, to be presented over four days – nine tragedies, three satyr plays, and five comedies, all new this year, selected from various submissions by a citizen jury and mounted at considerable expense by your democratic city with funds provided by wealthy families, who have vied with one another for the privilege of underwriting these public works, these 'liturgies' as they were called. At the end of the week there will be an awards ceremony, less flashy than the Oscars but somewhat along the same lines. But your feeling now is more like going to Mass than to the movies.

With perhaps sixteen thousand others you take your place in an outdoor theatre, a *theatron*, sacred to the god Dionysus. (Much of it survives today on the south slope of the Acropolis.)

It is still fairly dark as we take our places. Our stone seats, set into the side of the hill, form a vast semicircle, the arcs rising tier on tier. On the flat ground below (its paving gleaming in the darkness) is a circular area called the dancing place, the *orchêstra*. Because ours is a democracy, where every man is supposed to be good at every civic activity, many of us have performed on that *orchêstra*, trained to sing and dance by one of the playwright-composers. In the course of a year, some twelve hundred of us Athenian men perform at the dramatic festivals, and we take as much pride in doing that as we do in speaking in the assembly, serving on its committees, arguing in the agora, training in the gymnasia, fighting in the wars. We Athenians are good at a lot of things!

Beyond the *orchêstra*, its outlines hardly visible in the pre-dawn light, is the one building which will provide our scenery. The *skêne*. It represents, with painted panels, the royal house of whatever myth is being enacted. It has impressive central doors, and its interior can be revealed and even come sliding forward – like the sliding stages used today at the Metropolitan Opera.

Below us, the statue of the god Dionysus overlooks the playing area. The day before yesterday we escorted that statue in procession and, amid many sacrifices, set it in place. Yesterday, as the god watched, hundreds of us men and boys sang the myths of Dionysus in choruses of dithyrambs. And today, on ground consecrated to him, in the presence of his priest, we will see three plays by Aeschylus – four plays if you count the little satyr play that will send us out a little after noon with something of a smile. We need the satyr play because the three longer plays, stretching from dawn till high noon, are all trage-dies, telling one vast, overarching tale of gods and men, of terrible deeds and their punishment, of gods who pass away, of man's redemption, and of the eventual estab-lishment of a new order. (And if you think that is made to sound like Wagner's *Ring* cycle you have got the point.)

Tomorrow morning we will reassemble in the same fashion to see four more plays – three tragedies and a satyr play by one of Aeschylus's rivals. The day after that, we'll see, in the same fashion, four more plays – three tragedies and a satyr play by yet another playwright. The day after that, we'll reassemble for five more plays, all of them comedies, by five different comic writers. That is far more playgoing than any New Yorker or Londoner, or any tourist in those cities, is likely to undergo in a similar stretch of time. What made this easier to do in classic Athens was that you would only have to pay two obols (about ten cents) a day. And once Pericles took over the city you would have got in free – though when the long war with Sparta began things got a bit tight: you didn't have to pay at all, but you'd only be able to see fifteen plays in a mere three days of playgoing.

III

The *Agamemnon* begins in silence. On the roof of the *skêne* a single actor appears, leans his elbows on the rail, looks up at the still-dark sky overhead and speaks the prologue. We can hear his every whisper, because the acoustics in the theatre are phenomenal, and because he wears a mask of linen and cork which makes his voice resonate as it moves through its several registers. He is the watchman on the roof of King Agamemnon's palace. His king has been gone for ten years now. Will the war with Troy never end? The watchman has watched the stars:

> I ask the gods some respite from the weariness
> of this watchtime measured by years. I lie awake
> elbowed upon Agamemnon's roof dogwise to mark
> the grand processionals of all the stars of night
> burdened with winter and again with heat for men,
> dynasties in their shining blazoned on the air,
> these stars, upon their wane and when the rest arise.

Though this is a simple man speaking, the language does not strike us as altogether natural or simple. (The translation I am using, the famous 'Chicago' translation by Richmond Lattimore, attempts to preserve the flavour of the Greek, and not to prettify or clarify what is tough and knotty in the original.) What do we find in these opening words? From 'respite, weariness, watchtime' to 'wane and when the rest arise' there is an alliterative quality that takes some getting used to – unless you've heard

Wagner's *Ring,* with its pervasive alliteration. But more important are the images. Some of them are homely (the watchman is 'elbowed dogwise'); others are grand (the stars move in 'processionals ... dynasties in their shining, blazoned on the air'). We in the audience note the images carefully, for we know that Aeschylus is the finest imagist writing for our theatre, and we know that the images will soon begin to fall into patterns (as Wagner's musical motifs would centuries later) and that those patterns will (like Wagner's leitmotifs) be the best way to understand what the drama means.

Take the homely adverb 'dogwise,' that is, 'like a dog.' That image will eventually make a special kind of sense. What our Chicago man translates adverbially as '-wise' is, in Greek, '*dike,*' the noun commonly used for 'justice.' The use of '*dike*' to mean 'like' or 'in the manner of' is not exactly curious usage, but '*kunos diken,*' which our translator goes out of his way to render bluntly, is a curious phrase to find at the start of a tragedy. Why would Aeschylus want to use it?

Let us say, first, that Aeschylus's style is not always grandiose, and this is a common man speaking. But, more importantly, the theme of the trilogy is *Dike,* justice, and in each of the three dramas a character who perpetrates acts of violence will claim to have acted justly. Then as the trilogy ends, humanity moves to a new concept of justice. That theme is stated obliquely, in a startling phrase, as the drama begins.

More than that, the curious phrase almost inadvertently begins what will become a dominant image pattern throughout the trilogy. Every character in the three-part

drama will see himself, or herself, or the others, as dog or
eagle or ox or bull, as lion or serpent or swan. We might
cite, as a modern example of this, Ibsen's *The Wild Duck*.
Early in that play it is established that a wild duck, when
pursued by a hunter, will dive to the water's depths,
only to entangle itself in the seaweed and die. The wild
duck is clearly meant to be a symbol for someone in the
play, and as the four pivotal characters – Ekdal, Gregers,
Hedvig, and Hjalmar – are successively affected by reve-
lations of their various pasts, we who watch the drama
say, 'Oh, *he's* the wild duck ... No, *she's* the wild duck,'
until the action explodes in ironic but inevitable violence.
That pattern is not unlike the one Aeschylus uses in the
Oresteia. With its recurrent images of voracious birds and
beasts, and with additional patterns – arrows, nets,
yokes, the sea, the gleam of gold, the dripping of blood,
diseases and their dreadful emissions – all with reference
now to this character, now to that, the *Oresteia* is *The Wild
Duck* many times over.

So the watchman's homely image, 'dogwise' is not
without meaning. As for his grand image, about the
stars, 'processionals ... dynasties in their shining,' the
theatrical climax of the play to follow is the moment
when the head of a royal dynasty returns home in processional – to be murdered. Tragedy is always about
changes in fortune, and men's fortunes – their rise and
fall – are overseen in the cosmos, by those stars 'upon
their wane and when the rest arise.'

The watchman, in short, says a lot more than he
knows.

The speech goes on. The watchman on the roof is waiting for a light out of darkness. His queen, Clytemnestra, has arranged for a series of beacon fires to signal Agamemnon's return. When, across the sea, Troy is finally set afire, the news will be passed in a series of beacon fires, from mountain top to mountain top, from island to island, so that here in Greece the queen will know of the victory within minutes. Again the watchman's words begin a pattern of images. Light from darkness is an image that will recur over and over in the text. Eventually we, assembled in the early morning darkness, realize that Aeschylus has written his three plays so that this imagery reflects the sky over our heads. The first play, *Agamemnon*, starts in near darkness and is thick with metaphors we do not at first understand. During the second play, *The Libation Bearers*, morning lightens overhead, and the images in the text begin to thin out, the ideas to come clearer. In the third play, *The Eumenides*, there is virtually no obscurity in the language: the imagery has all but faded out of the text and become visible in the staging. And as the meaning of the trilogy comes clear, the sun reaches its high point in the sky above us.

'Light from darkness' is also fairly basic archetypal imagery. Robert Donington, writing on the opening scene of Wagner's *Ring*, where the Rhine's dark waters are suddenly illuminated by the gleam of the gold they contain, sees 'light from darkness' as an archetypal symbol for the male spirit of consciousness fertilizing the female unconscious. Aeschylus knows or at least intuits that: there is a lot in his trilogy, not just about light emerging from darkness, but about reconciling what today we would call male and female components in the human psyche. Even now the watchman is wondering about his queen's tyrannical nature. 'A lady's male strength of heart,' he says, is oppressing the people. And in fact, images of sexual ambivalence, the misbegotten actions of mannish women and womanish men, will propel Aeschylus's trilogy until all is resolved by a female deity who reconciles the two psycho-sexual aspects of human nature perfectly in her one numinous presence.

But just now, the watchman leaps up. He sees the beacon light, the signal that, across the sea, the Trojan War is over. 'Oh hail, blaze of the darkness,' he shouts, 'harbinger of day's shining, and of processionals ...' We turn in our seats and see a torch gleaming over our heads, at the highest row of the *theatron*. And the watchman speaks his joy in terms of rising and falling stars:

> I cry the news aloud to Agamemnon's queen,
> that she may rise up from her bed-of-state with speed
> to raise the rumor of gladness welcoming this beacon,
> and singing rise, if truly the citadel of Troy
> has fallen, as the shining of this flare proclaims.

But in a moment, his joy turns to foreboding. All is not well in the palace. He cannot say openly what he fears because 'an ox stands huge upon / my tongue.' The ox is of course Clytemnestra – that mannish woman who rules through terror. In the kind of proverb a simple man might use we have, combined, the soon-to-be pervasive patterns – a Wagnerian would say, the leitmotifs – of animal imagery and sexual ambivalence.

The watchman descends to the *skêne* to change his mask and costume. The actor who plays him will reappear later in two other roles. Tradition allows Aeschylus only three actors, all of them male, and each must play several roles in the course of the performance, changing costumes, masks, vocal registers, and acting styles.

But Aeschylus does have a dozen other performers at his disposal – his chorus. They now enter the *orchêstra*, to observe the rest of the action. The chorus members are ordinary citizens like us, trained by Aeschylus himself to mime, dance, and sing his verses. Most of a Greek tragedy was sung. We can tell by the metres that roughly one-third was declaimed, one-third was set to a measured speech-song, and one-third was sung in fully composed choral odes or in ensembles in which characters and chorus sang together.[6] The singing was very likely a unison or octave chanting of a single musical line,[7] accompanied by an reed instrument called the *aulos*, invariably called a flute by modern commentators, but more like the modern oboe – piercing in tone, and capable, when equipped with a second reed that acted as a drone, of considerable volume.[8] It was associated with the worship of Dionysus, as the lyre was with Apollo.

So, to the sound of the *aulos*, we see twelve choristers file in from the sides of the *theatron* across the circular *orchêstra*, richly dressed as elders of Agamemnon's court. Their song is about dark dreams that falter in daylight – for the daylight is breaking over our heads as we watch. The doors of the *skêne* open and the queen, Clytemnestra, enters the *orchêstra* silently. She is played by a male actor skilled in upper vocal registers, heavily costumed, with a huge, impassive mask. The only part of the actor's body we see are the hands. Clytemnestra is accompanied by silent attendants who advance to the altar – the *thymele* that is always set in the centre of the *orchêstra* – to light a sacrificial fire.

Then fires are lit all around the *theatron*, the flames leaping as the darkness overhead gradually turns to light. The chorus address urgent questions to Clytemnestra, but she (like Senta, Elisabeth, Elsa, Brünnhilde, and Kundry at their big moments in Wagner)[9] says nothing. At pauses in the music she turns her great masked face inscrutably towards us – and says nothing. The silence is sinister.

We do not have the musical score Aeschylus wrote, but the Greek text begins to fall into a musical structure – strophe, antistrophe, and epode. To the wailing sound of the *aulos*, the chorus sing, dance, and mime the events that happened earlier – the thousand ships assembled at Aulis, the rising of the crosswinds, the cruel decision of Agamemnon, and the piteous sacrifice of Iphigeneia. It is worth quoting some of their words, because Wagner was profoundly moved by this choral ode. In the last years of his life he returned to it frequently and said, 'One could write a whole book on it.' He asked his friend Wolzogen to do just that.[10] One evening in the summer of 1880, as Wagner's wife Cosima recalls it, 'Suddenly Richard remembers a long expressed desire of ours and calls for Aeschylus's *Agamemnon*. He then reads it, and I feel as if I have never before seen him like this, transfigured, inspired, completely at one with what he is reading; no stage performance could have a more sublime effect than this recital.'[11] Then the next morning she writes, 'Are impressions such as those of last night too powerful for poor mortals?' and adds, 'We luxuriate in memories of yesterday. R[ichard] says, "I declare that [chorus] to be the most perfect thing in every way, religious, philosophic, poetic, artistic."' Cosima says she would put only the *Ring* beside it. Wagner at first demurs, makes a feeble joke, and then, turning serious, says simply, 'It fits with my work.'[12]

To his dying day that choral ode was with him. At the end of Cosima's *Diaries*, her daughter Daniela added this note: 'Among Papa's last remarks were those he made at lunch ... when he said he had read Herr von Stein's article about the chorus in Aeschylus with great satisfaction. Regarding Aeschylus himself, he exclaimed "My admiration for him keeps on growing."'[13]

Here is one passage in the ode that impressed Wagner particularly:

> As eagles stricken in agony
> for young perished, high from the nest,
> eddy and circle
> to bend and sweep of the wings' stroke,
> lost far below
> the fledglings, the nest, and the tendance.

We said that the Trojan War began when Helen, the wife of Menelaus, was stolen away, and Agamemnon launched a fleet of ships to sail across the Aegean and bring her back. Here the two warrior-brothers are likened to a pair of eagles whirling over their airy nest after the loss of their young. We are alert enough to note the animal images, and the deliberately inexact identification of Helen as the eagle's young. We also note that sympathy is enlisted for the brothers in their loss. But perhaps most striking is the compression. Two similes are compacted in one. The brothers are compared to eagles, and the eagles are compared to ships. A lesser poet would say something like, 'The two brothers mourned the loss of Helen like two eagles that circle desolately over the nest when their young are lost,' and then add, 'The eagles fly overhead like ships that dip their oars in the foamy brine and sweep them across the blue expanses.' Aeschylus is more demanding. He states the two similes as one, and leaves the details almost impressionistic.

Then the ode tells how an omen encouraged Agamemnon and Menelaus to undertake their war against Troy. The two brothers looked up and actually saw two eagles,

> Kings of birds to the kings of the ships,
> one black, one blazed with silver ...
> they lighted, watched by all
> tore a hare, ripe, bursting with young unborn.

The brothers take this as a sign that *they* will tear open the walls of Troy and feed on its guilty people. But, the chorus goes on, Artemis, the virgin daughter of Zeus, a goddess 'lovely and kind' to the tender young of all animals, is 'angered with pity at the flying hounds' (the poet has metamorphosed his eagles) 'eating the unborn young in the hare and the shivering mother.'

So Artemis sends the crosswinds. Aeschylus describes the scene impressionistically:

... the crosswinds of fortune,
when no ship sailed, no pail was full ...
where the tides ebb and surge:
and winds blew from Strymon, bearing
sick idleness, ships tied fast, and hunger,
distraction of the mind, carelessness
for hull and cable.

Agamemnon's priest tells the father he must sacrifice his first-born, his daughter Iphigeneia. So now the portent of the eagles feasting is made to mean, not that the brothers will tear open Troy and destroy its inhabitants, but that they will destroy their own royal line, tearing apart in the act of so doing the mother who bore that first-born. The 'shivering mother,' as the omen is reinterpreted, is Clytemnestra.

Wagner didn't have Aeschylus's musical score or his choreographic plans, and even the words he read in a German translation. But the choral ode nonetheless fired his imagination and influenced him profoundly. Let us say, first, that it is thick with images that recur in subtle combinations and are constantly fluid, especially in their meanings. Wagner was fortunate to have Droysen's translation, which carefully preserved the images in their patterns and interrelations. (There was nothing comparable in English until the 'Chicago' translation we are using.) I have only suggested a few of the patterns here, and I've singled out the eagles because they are what Wagner was most taken with. That and the fact that the image patterns were set to music, and the music danced, and the mythic happenings mimed. This is a different kind of tragedy from Shakespeare's, where there is of course plenty of imagery deftly patterned, but where there is no deliberate attempt to be mysterious about it, and no elaborate music and dance to propel it.

In Shakespeare the dramatic emphasis is on action and character. In Aeschylus there is little action and even less characterization. Half of the play is given to the chorus, which ponders the action with words heavy with imagery that constantly shifts and suggests. The characters appear in dialogue just two or, very rarely, three at a time, and only at moments of high passion are there sudden bursts of action. In Aeschylus it is the chorus that really takes the stage and holds it. The other Greek dramatists, Sophocles and Euripides, started to change that. And Wagner liked them less. He could hardly tolerate Euripides at all. It was Aeschylus who obsessed him when he wrote the *Ring* text. It was Aeschylus he read in the afternoon through the years when he set the *Ring* to music in the morning. And in Aeschylus the real dramatic element is the chorus, interpreting in the *orchêstra* the real meaning of what the actors are acting in front of the *skêne*. The chorus sees everything at a deeper, intuitive, unconscious level while the actors hardly see anything at all, hardly know why they are acting as they do.

Wagner sensed that, and used it. There is no chorus in the *Ring* cycle, at least not till the last half of the last opera. Wagner decided to use, not a chorus in an *orchêstra* but an orchestra playing out of sight beneath the stage. It is there that the action of the operas he was henceforth to write receives its comment. That orchestral comment is made in musical themes – leitmotifs with the power of

Aeschylus's images, leitmotifs that carry the weight of associations, are constantly fluid, and used in subtle and powerful combinations. The orchestra in the mature Wagner operas knows more than the characters know, and ponders the meaning of the drama through ever-shifting musical images. So Wagner, reading Aeschylus aloud, said quietly and seriously, 'It fits with my work.'

IV

Cosima once asked Wagner why so many terrible things happen in Greek drama. His reply was, 'In order to make us aware of what life is.'[14]

Why there is evil in the world is one of the great questions asked and unanswered by philosophers, theologians, and – in the midst of their suffering – ordinary men and women. 'If God is good, why does he permit evil? Can God himself be evil? Why do we suffer? Why do the innocent suffer? Have our lives any meaning?'

In the next passage of the choral ode that affected Wagner so deeply, the elders, singing of 'bitterness in the blood, faith lost, terror like sickness,' ponder the problem of evil and wonder what God might be:

> Zeus, whatever he may be, if this name
> pleases him in invocation,
> thus I call upon him.
> I have pondered everything
> yet I cannot find a way,
> only Zeus, to cast this dead weight of ignorance
> finally from out my brain.

It might be said that there are three possible answers to the question 'What is it that directs the course of human events?' One could answer 'God' or 'Fate' or 'Chance.'

To that question Euripides, of the three Greek tragedians whose plays have come down to us, might give a different, and often cynical, answer in every new play, but eventually he would settle for 'Chance': nothing in the world is ordered; any observable ordering is only an illusion; everything happens by chance; the world is, in the end, meaningless.

Sophocles would answer, without hesitation, 'Fate': an impersonal, irreversible power has ordered and predestined everything, and nothing we can do will change it. The gods we worship cannot change the decrees of Fate; that is why they warn.

Aeschylus answers, 'God': 'Zeus, whatever he may be' directs the course of human lives. Whatever appearances of evil there may be in the world, eventually in the vast, overarching plan of Zeus (or whatever we might call him) good prevails. That is surely one reason why Aeschylus wrote in trilogies. In the course of the first play, we wonder, through evil upon evil. In the second, we come near to despair. But in the third, the goodness of a personal god, and the justice of his providential plan, comes clear. If we suffer, it is so that we may learn and grow. The chorus in the *Agamemnon* finds its answer in

Zeus, who guided men to think,
who has laid it down that wisdom
comes alone through suffering.

'That,' it will be objected, 'is hardly Wagner. It doesn't "fit" with his work. His *Ring* celebrates the *downfall* of the gods. In the end, in *Götterdämmerung*, the father god and all the other deities are consumed with fire, and the world is cleansed with water, and a new power – expressed only in a leitmotif sounding on the water and through the fire – is left to rule the world. Is that Aeschylus?'

Yes, I would say that it is.

In Aeschylus, there have already been two *Götterdämmerung*s. Long before Zeus, the chorus sings, there were two other father gods that, like stars, had risen and fallen. The first was Uranus, 'throbbing with gigantic strength.' He and his dynasty of cosmic gods ruled through violence and were destroyed. It is 'as if he never were, unspoken.' The world was taken over by Cronus, with his dynasty of Titans. He ruled through unreason and 'is gone.' Now there is Zeus, who rules, with his dynasty of Olympians, through reason.

At least two centuries before Aeschylus, the Greek poet Hesiod had detailed these mythic revolutions in the heavens in his *Theogony* (*Generations of the Gods*), and written another poem, *The Works and Days*, to caution the farmers who worked the earth of Greece that the worship of Zeus was their only hope for improving their humble lot. But the myths Hesiod tells reach back centuries before him. The three dynasties in heaven seem to represent three ages of man on earth. Prehistoric man, brutish and only vaguely aware of the world about him, worshipped Uranus and his cosmic gods, but had not the imagination to tell myths about them and so develop a theology. Then, with the first streaks of consciousness dawning, with full awareness of the titanic destructiveness of earthquakes and thunderstorms on the earth, man worshipped the son of Uranus, Cronus, and told the myth of how he slew his father and began to rule the world with force. Then, evolving into consciousness and reason, man worshipped, and placed his hope in, 'Zeus who guided men to think.'

That succession of dynasties is what I read in Aeschylus's ode, and it is not far from the way I read Wagner's *Ring* when I spoke of it on the air and in print.[15] The *Ring* 'fits' with Aeschylus. In fact, it *continues* Aeschylus. It moves on to the next evolutionary stage in human development. In the *Ring*, the god of reason and consciousness – Wotan, a Germanic Zeus – goes under as his predecessors had, and we face a future wherein a new (by Aeschylean count, a fourth) power will direct the world. From the leitmotif which is the only identification Wagner gives that power, the new force will be something akin to love, and it is already stirring within us. It has a feminine aspect, for the motif Wagner gives it was associated, in its only previous appearance in the *Ring*, with the father god's daughter. That is going beyond Aeschylus, continuing his theological view. But, as we shall see, it fits with his work.

The inevitable question in all of this is, 'Is it god that changes, or is it man that, evolving into higher states of awareness, changes his god?' That is the question pondered by the great choral ode that begins the *Agamemnon*, and it is central too to Wagner's *Ring*, with its dying father god and its divine dynasty marked for extinction. Small wonder that Wagner was thrilled by this opening chorus. It gave him the evolutionary ending he needed for his own *magnum opus* and a way to ponder, and suggest an answer for, one of mankind's great questions. The power that directs the course of human events is the god that man, at each stage of evolution, has realized.

V

But the sun's rays have at this point begun to streak the sky, as we watch the drama on the south slope of the Acropolis. Let me hurry through the rest of the action.

Clytemnestra hears from a messenger that most of Agamemnon's fleet has been destroyed on the return crossing.[16] So the king is virtually defenceless when, after ten years, he comes home in a shining processional: Clytemnestra has a rich crimson tapestry spread for him to walk on. There is a sinister splash of red across the *orchêstra* from the *skêne* where she stands to the place where his chariot halts. She invites him to trample that splendour underfoot. As he steps hybristically from his chariot, gloriously clad and larger than life (the actor's stature is enhanced by the high-soled buskins on his feet), he reveals a huddled figure in white – the Trojan princess Cassandra, whom he has taken as part of his spoil. The captive princess stays behind as the king walks across the splash of crimson and follows his queen into his palace. The tapestry is taken up and gathered within, and the doors of the *skêne* close.

Then comes a scene which Wagner, in the midst of writing the *Ring*, called 'the most perfect thing mortal art has ever produced.'[17] He once read it aloud with such passion that the painter Paul Joukovsky said, twenty-five years later, that Wagner's cry 'Apollo, Apollo' still resounded in his ears.[18]

Cassandra breaks a long silence,[19] steps from the chariot, and cries out:

Apollon! Apollon!

She begins to rave under the influence of the god who gave her the gift of prophecy. She dances wildly around the *orchêstra*, seeing in a vision all of the crimes committed in this royal house in the past. Then, dancing in wider circles and singing in a higher register, she describes what is happening in the house now:

To bathe bright with water ...
... the hand gropes now, and the other
hand follows in turn ...
Is it some net of death? ...
See there, see there! Keep from his mate the bull.
Caught in the folded web's
entanglement she pinions him and with the black horn
    strikes.

The chorus do not understand, for Cassandra's prophecies were never understood. But we, now sensitive to the images, we understand: inside, Clytemnestra has enmeshed her mate Agamemnon in his bath and is stabbing him to death, sacrificing him as one would a sacrificial animal, sacrificing him as once he sacrificed their daughter Iphigeneia.

Then Cassandra, dancing and singing in a frenzy, seems to see the terrifying crime committed in the palace in the past – prince Thyestes, deceived by Agamemnon's father Atreus, feeding on the flesh of his own children, and the Furies demanding blood for blood.[20] Then she sees the terrifying future: she herself will be killed when she enters the palace. She lifts her hands to the sun – to her god, Apollo, now rising overhead – and she walks through the doors to her death.

It is a scene to remind any Wagnerian of Sieglinde's hallucination in Act II of *Die Walküre* – where she envisions both the past destruction of her house and, in the future, the lethal attack on her Siegmund.

The chorus wonder about it all, and finally the doors of the *skêne* open again, and the interior slides forward; Clytemnestra appears in a tableau, standing over the bodies of her two victims, Agamemnon and Cassandra, wrapped in the crimson tapestry they were caught and killed in. Clytemnestra says that her act was just. Her effeminate lover Aegisthus supports her in her claim. The chorus, knowing now that the oppressive reign of the mannish queen and her womanish lover is stronger than ever, file out of the *orchêstra*. The sound of the *aulos* dies away.

By now it is 9:30 a.m. What is your reaction? Possibly it is one of the crowd reactions reported about dramatic performances of the fifth century BC by the comic writer Aristophanes: 'It's so *long*!' Or 'My bones ache, sitting on these stone seats.' Or 'There's that self-important member of the Boulê over there. I think I'll nip out, drop by his house while he's preoccupied here, and look in on his wife. We were sweet on each other once.' Or possibly, as you stretch and move about and buy something to eat from the vendors hawking olives and cheese, you say, 'I'll bet Aeschylus wins first prize with this one.' (He did.) Or 'I'll bet that crimson tapestry cost the city a drachma or two.' (It did.) Or 'He's changing Homer! He's inventing his own myth!' (He is.) Or, 'Did you notice how all the images in the text – the eagles, the lions, the arrows, the terrible thing dripping blood – were interacting and taking on new meanings as the play progressed?' (If you say that, you are Wagner's man in the theatre twenty-five centuries ago.)

VI

By 9:45 the second play is starting – the *Choephoroi* or *Libation Bearers*. This is the story familiar to operagoers from Richard Strauss's *Elektra*. It can be detailed quickly.

The chorus now are twelve captive slave women brought by Agamemnon from Troy. They have been ordered to pour libations of wine at his tomb to appease his spirit and to ward off the terrible dreams Clytemnestra has been having through the seven years since she murdered him. Justice, the libation bearers say, will turn the darkness to light.

At the tomb of their father, sister and brother meet: Electra, kept with the slaves in the palace, and Orestes, returned from his exile and determined to avenge his father's death. In the time-honoured manner of Greek tragedy, there is a recognition scene – brother and sister become aware each of the other's identity through a series of discoveries. Then, charged with the sense that their ancestors are watching them, they sing a passionate vengeance duet, 'bloody like the wolf,' steeling themselves for what must be done. The duet is almost half the play. Orestes, told that his mother has had a recurrent dream that she gave birth to a snake, resolves to 'turn snake to kill her.' I am reminded of those wolf's-breed brother and sister with the glancing mark of the serpent in their eyes – Siegmund and Sieglinde, in the first act of *Die Walküre*. But when Wagner read the impassioned duet aloud to Cosima, and she exclaimed over its 'surgings and its constant recurrences,' he said, 'I know something else like this. *Tristan und Isolde* in the second act.'[21]

Orestes leaves with his silent companion Pylades and kills Aegisthus offstage. Clytemnestra comes out of the palace and, despite the dream she has had – that the serpent she gave birth to sucked blood from her breasts – bares her breasts to her son and dares him to kill her. He hesitates – and Pylades, in the only line he has, says, 'What then becomes of the oracles declared by Apollo?' It is a striking moment, for we in the audience have assumed that this confrontation scene between mother and son will be a traditional *agon* between two characters, and that Pylades' is only a mute role. When, unexpectedly, Pylades speaks his solitary line, it is almost as if, suddenly, Apollo himself were speaking, demanding that his will be done. It is Apollo who has ordained that Orestes avenge his father by killing his mother. It is a terrible command to put upon a son, but that is all the justice Orestes, or even Apollo, knows so far.

Orestes takes his mother inside and fulfils Apollo's command. Then, as at the end of the first play, the doors of the *skêne* open again, and again on the sliding stage we

see a killer standing over the bodies of two victims –
Orestes standing over Clytemnestra and Aegisthus,
holding aloft the same crimson tapestry that had snared
his father years before, declaring that he too has acted
out of justice.

Finally, as the play ends, Orestes' mind gives way. He
who was marked with the sign of the serpent sees three
womanish serpentine figures (only he sees them) come
to demand in justice the death of the son who killed his
mother. He races across the *orchêstra* and out of the *theatron*.

It is 10:45. What do you say now as you rise and
stretch? 'This play has a lot less pondering and wondering from the chorus'? Or 'The ending was a shock!'? Or
'Did you notice that, by the end, all of the animal images
were subsumed in the one image of the serpent?' Or
'What kind of god is Apollo, who orders a son to kill his
mother? If blood keeps calling for blood, where will it
end?' That last is what the chorus of libation bearers sang
as the music faded away just now.

VII

By 11 a.m. we are ready for the third and final tragedy,
the *Eumenides*, or *The Kind Ones* – though at first the kind
ones are anything but kind. They are the chorus of this
third play – the three black-clad Furies risen from the
blood of the slain to feed on the blood of the slayer,
female monsters with serpents writhing in the hair of
their grotesque masks. The animal and the sexually
ambivalent image-patterns that were only in the text in

the first play, and had faded out of the text to become invisible characters, the Furies, in the second play, now appear visibly before us – three figures from the dynasty of gods before Zeus, survivors from a primitive age before the dawning of reason. They are so frightening in their appearance that, as an ancient (but not altogether trustworthy) 'Life of Aeschylus' records, the audience at one performance twenty-five centuries ago screamed in panic.

This sudden emergence of the daemonic and the irrational in what has seemed till this point classic (and so, presumably, enlightened) drama can come as a shock to those whose picture of Athens of the fifth century BC is one of abstract and rational thought, of idealized sculpture and chaste monumental architecture. But in fact the daemonic, the frightening, and the irrational lie at heart of Aeschylus's trilogy, and E.R. Dodds, in his pioneering study *The Greeks and the Irrational*, insists that 'the daemonic, as distinct from the divine, has at all periods played a large part in Greek popular belief.' Aeschylus, he says, 'did not have to revive the world of the daemons: it is the world into which he was born. And his purpose is not to lead his fellow-countrymen back into that world, but, on the contrary, to lead them through it and out of it ... by showing it to be capable of a higher interpretation, and, in the *Eumenides*, by showing it transformed ... into the new world of rational justice.'[22]

Set against the female Furies in this final play is the male Apollo. He too appears at last, one of the new dynasty of gods, representing the reign of reason. The panels on the *skêne* now represent his temple at Delphi.

Orestes has fled for sanctuary to the god who com-
manded him to avenge his father. But the ghost of the
murdered mother appears, to send the female Furies
after her son, to hound him across the earth. The *orchêstra*
is filled again with manic dancing as Orestes tries to
escape from his three pursuers.

Then, as the sun rises in the sky overhead, Aeschylus
moves the scene to the very place where we are sitting, to
the home of democracy, the acropolis at Athens. Orestes
has fled to *our* city. The old myth is going to be given a
new ending this morning.[23]

From the roof of the *skêne*, which now represents Athens, a radiant figure descends – Athena herself, splendid
with her spear and armour, come to hear both sides of
the dispute, to listen to the Furies, the old order that
wants Orestes destroyed, and to Apollo, the son of Zeus,
the new order that wants Orestes saved. The arguments
advanced are what a mythologist might call today archetypally female and archetypally male. Intuitive versus
rational. Familial versus political.

Neither side is right. A synthesis is needed. A jury of
twelve just citizens, that democratic Athenian invention,
is called to decide its outcome. The vote splits. Athena
herself must cast the deciding vote. And she does – for
mercy. Athena is, of course, the patron spirit of our Athens. She is also the deity who embodies in her one radiant person both the male and the female. Born fully
grown and fully armed from the brain of Zeus, she is the
feminine incarnation of male wisdom. She is the closest
Greek myth came to a second person of the Trinity – the
Logos, the father god's thought, his word sent to do his

will – and she is female. Wagner, centuries later, was to make her the Brünnhilde of his *Ring* cycle. Both Athena and Brünnhilde take the stage at the close of their massive trilogies to bring them to a conciliatory close, each of them the embodiment of her father's will.[24]

Athena in this final scene effects a kind of New Testament between god and man. The old gods punished blood with blood. Now her father Zeus will bring, through her, after a series of terrible happenings, a new concept of justice.

Athena speaks – and as she speaks Orestes is healed, and the curse on his family lifted. He leaves with Apollo, promising that his city will always be Athens's ally. The Furies, deprived of their prey, burst into a terrifying song, threatening – through strophe, antistrophe, and epode – to drop the venom of their hearts on Athens's soil, to rouse the winds of hate against the city, to tear Athens apart. (The eagles in the first choral ode, who could represent, in the successive dramas, Agamemnon and Menelaus, then Clytemnestra and Aegisthus, then Electra and Orestes, now seem really to have been emblematic of the Furies poised at the end to destroy civilization.)

Athena answers the song of the Furies with speech. But her speech works no spell. With every spoken argument she advances, the song of the Furies rises higher. Even her not-too-gentle reminder that she can wield the thunderbolts of her father Zeus fails to impress them.

Finally, Athena sings – and the Furies find themselves changing. Furies no longer, they feel themselves – through strophe, antistrophe, and epode – transformed to Eumenides, Kind Ones. As their venomous hate gives way, they promise the land of Athens fruitful fields, teeming flocks, prosperity, and peace. This final scene, where Athena's song turns unreasoning passion to reasoning compassion, is antiquity's supreme tribute to the power of music. And it is as wise as any of our modern psychiatries. Unreason, the dark unconscious, allegiance to familial as against tribal allegiances – those values of a prehistoric order that the Furies represent – ought not to be destroyed. They are values that a new, rational society like Athens should respect and preserve. No civilization can prosper under patriarchal, city-building, rational consciousness alone. In the end, the Furies are persuaded by music to pass beneath the hill where we are sitting, and live there, and communicate the intuitive wisdom of an older stage of civilization to our new democracy, Athens.

The trilogy ends, as we expect from Aeschylus, with a display of pageantry: the Kind Ones, no longer the furious enemies of Zeus but now his willing agents, change their black robes to crimson. (Perhaps they change their masks as well.) Athena leads them, torch in hand, in a shining processional across the *orchêstra* and out of the *theatron* till they pass out of sight to make their home under the nearby Areopagus, the place of Athens's ancient court of justice. The music of the *aulos* comes to a halt. Overhead the sun stands high in the sky of Zeus.

What do we say now as we rise from out seats? Perhaps that the crimson of the tapestry used to kill a king became the colour of the robes in which the Furies vested themselves to play a new, constructive role in a democracy. Perhaps that the ambivalent male-female pattern turned univalent and positive at the end, with the saving appearance of Athena, the female embodiment of the will of father Zeus.[25] And as for justice – justice is not any more the old law of blood for blood, not something mankind practised in prehistoric ages under older gods. Justice will come henceforth from a democratic court of law, and in the integration of the values associated archetypally with both female and male. (The essay Wagner was writing on the day he died was titled *Concerning the Feminine Element in the Masculine*.)

All of that is what I may be saying from my place here in the theatre of Dionysus. But over there they are saying that the trilogy has an explicitly political meaning, that it is a criticism of the recent decree that severely limited the powers of the Areopagus. And over there they are whispering that it is an attack on the assassins of the man who advocated this.[26] And over there they are quarrelling over the question of whether a person or a city can progress without acknowledging the irrational element in human nature and putting it to constructive purposes – a question Wagner's homely philosopher, Hans Sachs, ponders in *Die Meistersinger*. And over there they are asking, 'Is it the gods who change, or is it man who gradually learns more about himself, and so changes his gods?' – a question Wagner pondered as he wrote, and rewrote, and rewrote the last page of the text of *Götterdämmerung*. In other places, they are talking, as the crowd in a theatre always will, about the music and the dancing, the performances of the three versatile actors, the costumes and the production values.

Some of the audience may have begun to drift away, but most of us return to our places. Before we break for lunch, Aeschylus gives us the traditional satyr play. All the weighty problems he's posed for us we can ponder later. Just now, he presents us with a little light music and dance, perhaps even with a prank or two, and a prat-fall. For a half-hour, we watch the *Proteus* – a postlude about the *other* brother coming home from Troy, about Menelaus mastering the sea and returning with Helen for happ'ly ever-aftering, all of it spun on by a chorus of half-men, half-beasts. It is a celebration of the origins of tragedy (goat-song) in the sacrifices to Dionysus.

The text for the *Proteus* has not been preserved for us, but we do know that the young Wagner, influenced by his knowledge of classical drama, first conceived of *Die Meistersinger* as a sort of satyr play to be performed after the three acts of his tragic *Tannhäuser*. And, Wagner being Wagner, that little satyr play, when he turned to it, became the longest, and in some ways the most pro-found, of all his works.

CHAPTER TWO

Intermission

Before we move on to Wagner, a few final words about Aeschylus. We have nothing like an authentic biography from antiquity, but we can piece together some details of his life from various sources. He was born into an aristocratic family in 525 BC, at a time when Athens was moving from aristocracy to democracy, opening up commercially, and enthusiastically developing its arts. Aeschylus fought the invading Persians at the battle of Marathon (490 BC), where his brother was killed clinging to an enemy ship as it pulled away from shore. He may have fought in the decisive naval battle with the Persians at Salamis (480 BC) as well: he describes it in clearer detail in his play *The Persians* than any of the contemporary historians do in their histories. He loved his Athens, and had an abiding hope for the future of its emerging democracy. It is clear that he thought deeply, too, about his religious heritage, and strove to make the old myths of his gods intelligible and relevant to the Athens of his day, which, we gather from the plays, he saw as hybristically overconfident.

But above all he was a man of the theatre. He composed his own texts and his own music, did his own directing, staging, and choreography, and, at least at first, acted and sang in his own dramas. He was the complete dramatist, and his art was the prototype of what Wagner was later to call the *Gesamtkunstwerk* – the 'complete work of art' that combined the separate arts of poetry, drama, dance, music, and painting in a communal exploration of ethical, political, and religious ideas. Aeschylus's name was synonymous in Athens with magnificence – magnificence of language, imagery, costuming, and staging. Some thought he overdid the magnificence. There was much more music in his dramas than in those of his rivals Sophocles and Euripides. But we are told (Plutarch, *On Music* 1137d) that it was simpler than theirs, majestic and invariably diatonic.

Though in his thirty-year career he won thirteen annual awards at the dramatic festivals, and Pericles, the greatest statesman of classic Athens, was once his chorus leader, he had his critics. And Athens did not, after his death in 456 BC, heed his warnings. It went on its aggressively imperial way, and it came to disaster in the long war against Sparta. Of his more than eighty plays, only seven have come down to us complete – *The Suppliants*, *The Persians*, The *Seven Against Thebes*, *Prometheus Bound* (the authenticity of which is questioned), and the three parts of the *Oresteia*. Quotations from some of the other plays are also extant, as well as fragments of his choral lyrics, elegies, and epitaphs.

Because his plays were largely sung, it might be of interest to quote from what little remains to us from the music of ancient Greece. We have lost much from the fall of ancient civilizations. Of the thousand tragedies produced at Athens in its golden age we have only thirty-six surviving in virtually complete form. Of the hundreds of poems of the poetess Sappho we have possibly one complete. We've lost the great chryselephantine statues of Pheidias, and all the dialogues of Aristotle that might have proved him as great a literary artist as Plato. But the saddest loss of all is the loss of virtually all of the music of ancient Greece. Only one piece has survived intact, and that is short and late, five centuries after Aeschylus. There are some sixty other remnants, fragments all, preserved on stone or papyrus, or copied in manuscripts in later ages. (The authenticity of many of the latter has often been called into question.)

Luckily some ancient treatises on Greek music have come down to us, and a fourth-century AD table for decoding the musical notation which appears as small alphabet characters above the texts, or, in the rare case of instrumental melodies, as a simple row of such letters. The oldest music from Greek antiquity (and one of the newest discovered) is instrumental, on a black-figure painting from the sixth century BC, preserved in the museum at Eleusis: an Amazon calls her comrades to battle by sounding a brass instrument, and circling around her are painted the five notes of her fanfare – in modern notation C-C-G̲-C-E̅.[1]

In recent years a musical scholar in, I'm happy to say, Nuremberg has, like the mastersingers of old, classified for us all the subsequent fragments and transcribed them into modern notation.[2] So I am emboldened, as Wagner's musical amateur Walther von Stolzing was emboldened by Nuremberg's Hans Sachs, to reproduce here the one complete piece of ancient Greek music that survives, as well as the fragment that is most germane to our purposes.

The complete piece, the so-called 'Skolion (Drinking Song) of Seikilos' is only four lines long and, dating from around AD 150, very likely much different from any of the music of Aeschylus. But since its discovery on a small cylindrical grave marker in Turkey in the year Wagner died, 1883, it has become the most widely known piece of ancient Greek music.[3] As in so many Greek epitaphs, it is the dead person who is speaking from the tomb to us, the passersby:

Ho - son zēs, phai - nou,

mē - den ho - lōs___ su lu - pou,___

pros o - li - gon es - ti to zēn,___

to te - los ho chro-nos ap - ai - tei._____

As long you live, be radiant.
Let nothing at all cause you pain.
Life lasts but a little.
Time will take away everything in the end.

We have no way of knowing whether that melody should be rendered *piano* or *forte*, *allegro* or *adagio*, diatonically, chromatically, or enharmonically – the three modal styles of ancient Greek music. When sung *piano, adagio,* and – as is the mode used in music today – diatonically,[4] the tune comes out mournful and memorable. The text and music are 'signed' on the grave marker 'Seikilos Euter' (that is perhaps to say, 'By a Sicilian son of [the Muse] Euterpe'), to which there is added the one word 'Zē' – 'he lives.' Seikilos has survived the person, perhaps the wife, who bids him live radiantly through the rest of the life that remains to him.

Among the sixty or more authenticated and unauthenticated ancient musical fragments preserved for us, two, on papyrus, have been positively identified as being by Aeschylus's near contemporary Euripides. The first of these comprises only forty-seven scattered notes written over a choral ode from his *Orestes*; the other is a sustained musical line written over a quotation from his posthumously produced *Iphigeneia at Aulis.*

And one of the other fragments may be by Aeschylus himself. It was discovered in 1918, on the reverse side of a papyrus containing a second-century AD Roman military document. Though the papyrus is now kept in Berlin, the attribution of the fragment to Aeschylus's lost play *Hoplôn Krisis (The Judgment of the Armour)* was first made in Toronto, at this university, by the late Professor F.M. Heichelheim.[5] The fragmentary words of this piece are addressed to the Greek warrior Ajax, who fought at Troy and killed himself with his father's sword when the arms of the slain Achilles were awarded, not to him as expected, but to the wily Odysseus. The piece has come to be known as 'Tecmessa's Lament,' and indeed it is possible to envision Tecmessa, the captive lover of Ajax, singing the lines as she stands over his corpse with the sword in her hand, cursing Odysseus and watching the blood seep from her beloved's wound and fall to the black earth:

Au - to-pho-nō   che - ri   kai   phas - ga - non

Te - la-mō - ni - a - da,   to son, Ai   -   an,

di O - dus - e - a   ton a - li - tron, ho

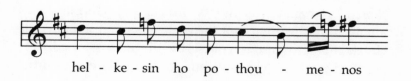

hel - ke - sin   ho   po - thou   -   me - nos

With suicidal hand ...
Ajax, your father's sword ...
because of traitor Odysseus, who still lives ...
with your wound ...
<you> beloved, lost to me ...

Wagner could not have heard either of those pieces, and it is doubtful whether he heard even the four pieces of ancient Greek music that were known in his day. These are attributed to Mesomedes of Crete – two hymns to Apollo and one each to Calliope and Nemesis, written at the time, and perhaps at the court, of the emperor Hadrian (76–138). They were known to the scholar Girolamo Mei (1519–94), passed on to Vincenzo Galilei (father of the astronomer), and published by him in his *Dialogue of Ancient and Modern Music* (1581). It is unlikely that either man could decipher the notation, but Galilei was a member of the Florentine Camerata, that group of classicists which produced, enthusiastically, what are regarded as the first operas – Jacopo Peri's *Dafne* (1597) and *Euridice* (1600). The simple monodic quality that characterizes these evolutionary operas was probably the direct result of what Galilei was able to tell the Camerata, from the four fragmentary pieces of Mesomedes, of the nature of classic Greek music.[6]

But it is hard to imagine any music farther from the complexities of Wagner's mature works than these skeletal remains. The nineteenth-century German was inspired by the ideal, not the archaeological remains, of Greek music – and of course by the impassioned network of words, ideas, and images in the Greek dramas which survived, and which he read in wonder.

CHAPTER THREE

Brünnhilde Sings

Wagner was not the first, or the last, revolutionary to take up his schoolroom Greek books again and use Greece as a rallying cry. The revolutionary fathers of the United States, Thomas Jefferson in particular, thought of making Attic Greek the official language of their politics and diplomacy – an idea, it was realized all too soon, that was utterly impracticable. Wagner, like those Hellenizing Americans, never succeeded in mastering classical languages, but his Greek ideas stayed with him long after his revolutionary ideas, political and artistic, had faded. The aging conservative who wrote *Parsifal* was still alive to the spirit of Greece, and he exclaimed over the greatness of the first chorus of the *Agamemnon* the day he died.

But let us begin with the schoolroom. At the age of nine, Wilhelm Richard Geyer, as Wagner was known then, from his stepfather's name, entered the Dresden Kreuzschule and, as Ernest Newman reports, 'applied himself very casually to the subjects that did not interest him' and 'made no exceptional progress in those that did, because of his congenital disability to learn except in his own way ... He was attracted to Greek because his imagination had been stirred by stories from Greek mythology and he wanted to recreate those dramatically according to his own vision of them.'[1] But he was impatient with Greek grammar and syntax, and he actively disliked Latin. One of his masters, Karl Julius Sillig, urged him to make philology his profession – an understandable suggestion at first, for the otherwise unpromising Richard Geyer would volunteer German translations of the Greek poets he liked, all done into the appropriate metres. But there were vast areas of classical studies that only looked like so much desert to him.

Homer he loved – how could he not? He was only human. In his autobiography *Mein Leben* he records that, under Magister Sillig, he had the honour of reciting before the class both Hamlet's 'Sein oder nicht sein' and Hector's 'Lebwohl' to Andromache from Book 6 of the *Iliad*. He also remarks almost casually that he translated twelve books of Homer into German in a single school year – and indeed the records at the Kreuzschule do show that only Richard Geyer of all the boys in class submitted a translation of the first three books of Homer's *Odyssey* in the Michaelmas term of 1826. Did he really do nine more in the next term? It seems unlikely, for soon the young Wagner had to move to a different city – back to Leipzig, where he was born – and enrol in another and then yet another school, and fell behind in his studies, and was demoted to a lower form. He was humiliated and surly, especially when, assigned in fifth form to write a poem, he 'produced a chorus in Greek about the most recent war of liberation' which, he says, 'was scornfully rejected as an effrontery.'[2] When he was dismissed from school without a hope of entering university, he turned away from the classics.

Meanwhile, his uncle, Adolf Wagner, a scholarly but long-winded translator and man of letters, took the difficult young man along on his afternoon constitutionals, gave him access to his library, and read with him his own translation of Sophocles. To the end of his life Wagner

was grateful to him. And twice more, at age seventeen
and again at twenty-seven, he tried to master classical
Greek thoroughly. He failed. In the first instance, the
smell from a tannery across the street from the house
where he was being tutored made it impossible for him,
an impatient adolescent, to concentrate. In the second,
when he was a married man eking out a pauper's existence in Paris, he was told by Samuel Lehrs, the kindly
but equally impoverished Jewish scholar who undertook
to read Homer with him, that he had by then too much
music in him to learn Greek thoroughly.

Lehrs died of consumption at thirty-seven. Wagner,
pronouncing his relationship with Lehrs 'one of the most
beautiful friendships of my life,'[3] returned to Dresden
and proceeded to educate himself in knowledge of all
kinds, and by the age of thirty he had amassed a library
of over four hundred volumes that was, he said, as
important to his work as was his piano.[4]

Wagner's early operas were based on Gozzi (*Die Feen*)
and Shakespeare (*Das Liebesverbot*) and owe nothing to
the Greek theatre. The next, *Rienzi*, based on Bulwer-
Lytton, was historical in subject, and *The Flying Dutchman* mythic, and *Tannhäuser* and *Lohengrin* increasingly
sophisticated combinations of the historical and the
mythic. But, for all the real accomplishments in the last
three works especially, there is no indication in them that
Wagner thought of them in Greek tragic terms. Later, in a
prose work called *A Communication to My Friends* (1851),
he was to say that the last three owed their power to
being German equivalents of Greek myths, that the Flying Dutchman was a figure similar to Homer's wander-

ing Odysseus, that Venus in *Tannhäuser* was a Circe, that Elsa in *Lohengrin* was a Semele. But he never claimed that he had those specific myths in mind, not even in his subconscious mind, when he wrote. And I don't think that he did.[5]

It was not till Wagner was thirty-four, finishing the scoring of *Lohengrin*, that Greece came back to possess him, and with far greater force than before. He read Droysen's German translation of and commentary on Aeschylus, and wrote, 'I could see the *Oresteia* with my mind's eye as if [it were] actually being performed, and its impact on me was indescribable. There was nothing to equal the exalted emotion evoked in me by [the] *Agamemnon*, and to the close of *The Eumenides* I remained in a state of transport from which I have never really returned to become fully reconciled with modern literature.'[6]

Classical scholarship of the day treated Greek drama almost exclusively as a vehicle for the study of language, as philology. Wagner, with 'too much music in him' now to learn Greek, *visualized* Greek drama as he read it, imagined its music and dance, responded to it as an energetic, politically involved Athenian might have. His artist friends in Dresden were suddenly surprised to find him talking about Greek literature instead of his *Lohengrin*. The Austrian poet Johannes Nordmann said, after a visit with Wagner, 'He talked about the Greek dramatists with a sympathy and understanding one would look for in vain among some university professors.'[7] He thought of writing incidental music for Euripides' *Helen*, of an opera on Achilles, of a drama on Alexander the Great.

None of these projects materialized. Wagner had to flee to Switzerland when the Dresden uprising failed. There, an exile reft of his precious library, he bought a copy of Homer, began reading him for the first time since his boyhood, and was deeply moved. E.M. Butler in her book *The Tyranny of Greece over Germany* tells how Goethe, Schiller, Hölderlin, and the rest lived their intellectual lives in the light and shadow of ancient Greece. So, from his thirty-fourth year until the day he died, did Richard Wagner.

II

Despite the forceful suppression of the 1849 uprising in Dresden, Wagner still hoped that Germany's oppressive rulers, its old gods, would, like those of the *Ring* he was contemplating, go under, and that his country would be reorganized along democratic lines – with himself as the guiding cultural force. In Zurich, a place where other intellectual revolutionaries have sat out their exiles, Wagner began to commit his subversive ideas to paper. He may not have had the political savvy of his friend Mikhail Bakunin, the Russian anarchist who was one of the leaders of the uprising, but his ideas at the time were, in their way, as anarchic – nothing much short of destroying his Germany to build on the ruins a new Germanic version of classic Greece:

The public art of the Greeks, which culminated in the tragedy, was the expression of the deepest and noblest

elements in the national consciousness; the deepest and
noblest elements in *our* consciousness express themselves
in quite the opposite way – in the refusal to produce any
public art at all.

To the Greeks the presentation of a tragedy was a religious festival ... *our* theatre has so low a place in public
esteem that it becomes the business of the police to forbid
it to touch on religious themes – and this tells us a good
deal about both our religion and our art.

In the vast spaces of the Greek amphitheatre the whole
citizenry could be present; in *our* aristocratic theatres
there are only the well-to-do, idling away their time ...

The education of the Greek made him from his earliest
youth the object of his own artistic efforts, body and soul;
our stupid educational system, geared as it is mainly
toward future industrial profit, instils an absurd and even
arrogant disdain for art.

The Greek was actor, singer, and dancer, and participation in a tragic performance was to him an honour to be
won by his beauty and training; *we* allow a certain element of our proletariat to be instructed for our entertainment, and the ranks of our theatre people are filled with
dissolute idlers, pleasure-seekers, opportunists looking
for a quick road to riches ... Greek art was really art. Ours
is pseudo-artistic craftsmanship.

That and more from *Art and Revolution* (1849) provides a
vivid picture, not just of 'the tyranny of Greece' over the
disillusioned Wagner, but of a mind arguing its way to
an artistic creed. It was a mind which saw Athenian

drama as the supreme achievement of all past civilizations, the political and religious expression of a unified
polis whose art was in its blood and sinews.

Above all, Greek drama was to Wagner an art form in
which all the arts converged on a single purpose. It was,
to use his word, a *Gesamtkunstwerk*, an art form to which
all the arts contributed, performed by the people it spoke
to, providing them with new insight into their ancestral
myths, integrating them anew into the life of their city.
The arts reached their greatest expressive power, Wagner
thought, in interdependence, and this had happened
only once, only for a few decades, in Greece. Then, with
the breakup of the Greek city state and the decline of
drama, the arts no longer conspired together:

> Rhetoric, sculpture, painting, music, and the rest aban-
> doned the roles they had played together. Each went its
> own way, self-sufficient but isolated, to continue its own
> development. Each ... has since filled the world with a
> wealth of harvest. In each, geniuses have worked mira-
> cles. But the one true art was not revived, not by the
> Renaissance or by any age since – the *Gesamtkunstwerk*,
> the great integrated expression of a free community, the
> drama.[8]

Wagner saw it as his role not to revert to but to recreate
in his own time that long-lost art form, even if it required
a new Germany in order to achieve it. He had hopes that
a major revolution would begin in France and spread
across Europe, destroying both aristocracy and moneyed
classes and clearing the ground for a free Germany to be

revitalized and nourished, as Athens once was, by its theatre. Another, much longer, prose work appeared, *The Art-Work of the Future* (1850). The tone is more wide-eyed than before:

> Let us look to the wonderful art of Greece, and when we have seen deeply into it, let us understand how the art of the future must be created. Nature has done all that she could do. She has produced the Greeks, nourished them at her breast, formed them with her mother's wisdom. Now with a mother's pride she sets them before us, and with a mother's love she cries to all mankind: 'This I have done for you. Now, of your love for one another, do what *you* can.'[9]

This new essay attempts a panoramic overview of Greek literature that culminates in a hymn to one of Wagner's favourite abstractions, *das Volk*. In spite of the philistine treatment he had theretofore received, he was sure that 'the people' would rally to his cause. He believed rather naively in the innate goodness and sound artistic instincts of ordinary people who were still unspoiled by the political decadence of his Europe. He was to be bitterly disappointed in the German *Volk*, but his idealized view of them was eventually to find beautiful and persuasive expression in *Die Meistersinger*.

When Wagner's new hopes for revolution were dashed by Napoleon II's *coup d'état* in 1851, he was working on his most ambitious prose work, *Opera and Drama*. Now the revolutionary fever dies out in the prose, and in long, convoluted sentences, filling hundreds on hun-

dreds of pages, Wagner begins to articulate what he feels
about the roles of song and speech in drama. Opera, he
says, is potentially the greatest art form of all, even if the
opera of the day knows nothing of myth or religion and
serves no purpose in the community other than to foster
idle aestheticism and empty musical display. For real
drama, he turns to the past works of Shakespeare,
Racine, Goethe, Mozart, and Beethoven – but in the end
the formative impulse is again his vision of Greece. In
the new as in the Greek theatre, all the arts will work
together to create the drama. And the dramatic material
will always be drawn from myth, because in myth 'man
apprehends, without knowing it fully, his own self.'
Myth is the ideal subject matter for the dramatist because
it comes from *das Volk*. It is, to put it in more contemporary terms, archetypal: it comes from what Jung calls the
collective unconscious. Speaking of the story of Oedipus,
Wagner says, 'The wonderful thing about this myth is
that it is always true. What it says, in concise form,
remains inexhaustible for all ages.' Long before Freud,
Wagner wrote, 'Today we have only to interpret the
Oedipus myth in a way that keeps faith with its essential
meaning to derive a coherent picture of human nature
itself.'[10]

Also in *Opera and Drama* some important decisions are
made about how, in the future, Wagner will use voices
and instruments. The singers will speak their music,
along the lines set by the actors in Greek drama. The
orchestra will interpret their words on a deeper – in
today's terminology, on a subconscious – level, along the
lines of the chorus in Greek drama. As this new promi-

nence of the orchestra is so striking a feature of Wagner's work, perhaps the one feature that those who come to Wagner from Verdi or Mozart find most difficult, it may be profitable to move ahead nine years to another prose work, *The Music of the Future* (1860), for his best statement on it:

> The orchestra will have much the same relation to my sort of drama as in Greece the chorus had to the tragic action. The Greek chorus was always present in the playing area. The motives of the drama lay open before its eyes, and it sought to penetrate those motives and form from them some judgment on the action. But the participation of the Greek chorus was generally of a reflective nature; it remained apart from both the action and the motives. The orchestra in my modern symphonic drama will participate so intimately in the motives of the action that it alone, and not the singers, will give the music definite shape. And it will keep that music in an endless flow in order to communicate what the drama means.[11]

So the famous (or, depending on your point of view, notorious) aspects of Wagner's mature music dramas – mythic stories, philosophic texts, a strange kind of speech-song replacing conventional arias and duets, and an orchestra of endless, surging melody commenting on the action, engulfing and sometimes overwhelming the singers – all of these elements are consistent, and to an extent evolved from, Wagner's idea of Greek drama. It is not that Wagner wanted to revert to Greek drama, or re-create it. He wanted to go beyond it. He fully acknowledged that the great German musical tradition of the century that had preceded him, Beethoven especially, gave him the opportunity to surpass even the finest things the Greeks had done. 'Ehrt eure Deutschen Meister,' sings Hans Sachs at the end of *Die Meistersinger*. And honour his German masters Wagner did, as he faced the future.

III

After six years of such theorizing, Wagner turned at last to composing again. The ideas were tested. They work very well indeed in *Das Rheingold*, achieve their highest expression in the first act of *Die Walküre*, and carry on through the rest of that work, through the first two acts of *Siegfried* and, when progress on the *Ring* was interrupted, into *Tristan und Isolde* up to the point at the end of Act I when Wagner decided to let the two lovers blend their voices.

On the face of it, nothing about these mature works may seem Greek. But consider, first, the text of the *Ring* – four massive dramas which Wagner for decades persisted in calling, not a tetralogy, but a trilogy with a preliminary evening. He was still convinced that, as the Greek dramatists had presented their tragedies in groups of three, and as Aeschylus at least had developed the same myth through the three dramas, that was the proper way for him to proceed.

At the start, it was not Wagner's intention to write an Aeschylean trilogy. He wanted to dramatize the injustices of the political situation of his Europe, and suggest

a solution for them, and he thought myth the most powerful – in more modern terms, the most archetypal – way
of doing so. He chose for his purpose the *Nibelungenlied*,
a thirteenth-century High German epic in which the
Rhenish hero Siegfried woos the Icelandic queen Brünnhilde for a Burgundian king and is then done in by the
king's villainous vassals. The long poem had achieved
new popularity in Wagner's day. Though it was set in a
legendary Christian Europe, he proceeded to transfer it,
effectively, into the pre-Christian past where it had been
told in its earlier forms. But before setting any of that
story to music, he decided that it needed to be prefaced
with a drama drawn largely from the thirteenth-century
Norse-German *Thidreks Saga*, in which the young Siegfried kills a dragon and wins a Rhineland treasure. That
in turn needed to be prefaced with an adaptation of the
Icelandic *Volsunga Saga* – the most important of the
sources – which told in prose of the hero Sigurd's parents
Siegmund and Sieglinde and their fathering by the sky
god Odin (Wotan). And finally Wagner decided to intro-
duce all of this material with details from the Scandina-
vian *Poetic Edda* and *Prose Edda* which, though written in
the Christian era, provided other stories of the old pagan
gods. There was some overlap from source to source, and
Wagner made use of some lesser materials as well before
he published the texts of his four dramas – now arranged
so that the events would unfold in a continuous story
and titled *Das Rheingold, Die Walküre, Siegfried*, and *Götterdämmerung*.

Readers familiar with the *Nibelungenlied* in Wagner's
day (it was being belatedly hailed as the German

national epic) must have been surprised by the many changes Wagner made in the story, perhaps most surprised that Brünnhilde, the amazonian queen of Iceland, had become the daughter of the father god Wotan, and that Siegfried had been conflated with the Sigurd of the *Volsunga Saga* and so given a divine ancestry as well. Shaping his legendary medieval material into a single compelling narrative[12] and transplanting it to a pre-Christian world had posed problems which Wagner surmounted in spectacular ways. And three of the most important of these seem to have been inspired by his reading of the Greek classics.

Consider this: Wagner begins his cycle with Alberich's primeval theft of the gold from the bottom of the Rhine. There is no such incident in the old sagas – but in the Prometheus trilogy, as it was reconstructed in Wagner's day,[13] the action begins with Prometheus's primeval theft of fire from heaven.

And consider this: Wagner's thief, when he himself is the victim of thievery, puts a curse on the gold and all those who will possess it, and that curse operates through the trilogy of dramas that follow, only to be lifted at last when the sky god's daughter, in self-immolation, brings into the world a new rule of love. There is none of this in Wagner's sources – but in Aeschylus's *Oresteia*, as we have seen, a curse operates throughout the trilogy, affecting every generation of the house of Atreus, only to be lifted when the sky god's daughter appears, to establish in Athens a new concept of justice.

And consider this: Wagner, linking his Siegfried myths with the quite separate myth of the Twilight of the Gods, has Zeus and his dynasty fade away at the end of the *Ring*, to be superseded by a new power, expressed by a radiant musical theme sounding through the cleansing fire and water. In the old Norse myth of *Ragnarök*, no such power emerges to rule the world; the gods battle the powers of evil, all the combatants on both sides are slain, and the world is consumed by cosmic fire. But, as we have seen, Aeschylus in the great choral ode in the *Agamemnon* tells how two dynasties of Greek gods have passed away, to be superseded by 'Zeus, whatever he may be' – a new power that promises justice.

In short, Wagner found a beginning for his cycle in a theft like that in *Prometheus*, the means of binding his long story together in a curse like that in the *Oresteia*, and the means of bringing the cycle to an end in the emergence of a new power like that hymned in the great ode in the *Agamemnon*.[14]

And there is much more. In 1933 Arthur Drews, a professor of philosophy at Karlsruhe University, published a piece in the progam booklet of the Bayreuth festival which argued that the *Prometheus* trilogy, as reconstructed by Droysen, had provided Wagner with some of the most striking details in the *Ring* – the visit to Nibelheim, the underworld abode of the dwarfs where the gold is forged into a ring that will enslave the world (Prometheus, in one of the partially surviving plays of Aeschylus, sees Hephaestus forging the chains that will imprison the Titans); the appearance of the goddess Erda from out of the earth (Prometheus's mother is the earth goddess Gaia); and, most importantly, Wotan's binding Brünnhilde on her rock in a ring of fire (Zeus decrees that

Prometheus be bound to his rock by the fire god Hephaestus). None of these Promethean scenes, so effective in Wagner's operas, occur in his Norse and Germanic sources.[15]

Drews's piece seems to have attracted little attention at the time. But thirty years later, Wagner's grandson Wieland, sure that there was still more of Greece in his grandfather's work, invited a renowned classical scholar, Wolfgang Schadewaldt, to write a series of pieces on Wagner and the Greeks for the Bayreuth programs. Even Wieland must have been surprised by what Schadewaldt found: Wagner was, consciously or unconsciously, indebted to Greek authors for any number of details in his operas, particularly in the *Ring*, where Homer provides much of the characterization: the Wotan and Fricka who appear in the *Ring* are – especially in their *Walküre* wrangling – Germanic versions of Zeus and Hera in the *Iliad*. Brünnhilde, an Icelandic virago in Wagner's sources, becomes in the *Ring* a Homeric *Speerjungfrau*, an Athena, the warlike daughter of the father god, the feminine embodiment of his masculine will, hastening to the aid of Siegmund when he fights Hunding as Athena hastens to help Achilles when he fights Hector, cleansing the guilt of past misdeeds at the end of the *Ring* as Athena does at the end of Aeschylus's *Oresteia*. Schadewaldt doesn't say much about Siegfried, who in the course of the *Ring* becomes a sort of hero manqué. (Wagner's interest had shifted to Wotan, whom he came to see as the really tragic figure in the cycle.) But I've often thought that Wagner felt compelled to give his diminished hero a massive funeral march and fiery funeral pyre because

Homer had so honoured Patroclus and Hector in the *Iliad*.

And Schadewaldt doesn't mention what to me is the most frightening use of Homer in the *Ring* – the moonlit appearance of Alberich in Hagen's dream at the start of the second act of *Götterdämmerung*. 'Schläfts du, Hagen mein Sohn?' ('Are you sleeping, Hagen my son?'), Alberich begins. Hagen, who appears to be dreaming but has his eyes open, enters into dialogue with the dream figure, which repeats, at the end of each of his fearsome injunctions, 'Schläfts du, Hagen mein Sohn?', and eventually fades into the darkness with the repeated warning, 'Sei treu!' ('Be true'). Dream apparitions of this sort occur in both of Homer's epics. At the start of Book 2 of the *Iliad*, Zeus sends an evil dream to Agamenmon; it takes the shape of Nestor, begins, 'Are you sleeping, son of wise-hearted Atreus?', gives its counsel, and ends, 'Hold this in your heart.' At the start of Book 23 the ghost of Patroclus appears to the slumbering Achilles; it begins, 'Do you sleep, Achilles, forgetful of me?' and, departing, implores, 'Give me your hand.' And at the end of Book 4 of the *Odyssey*, Athena sends a phantom to Penelope; it appears as her sister Iphthime, begins, 'Are you sleeping, Penelope, stricken in your heart?' and engages in a dialogue with the sleeper before gliding through the latched bedroom door onto the breath of the winds.[16]

Homer apart, Schadewaldt found that much of the action in *Das Rheingold* was derived from – it should come as no surprise – the *Prometheus*. Not only was Alberich's theft of the Rhine's gold suggested by Prometheus's primal theft of fire, but the important early

appearance of the Rhine maidens, who are at most incidental in the sources,[17] seems to have been suggested by
the arrival of the Oceanids who come to comfort the
bound Prometheus, and the giants' building of Valhalla
to have been suggested by the Titans' building (in Droysen's reconstruction of the *Prometheus* trilogy) of the cas-
tle of Zeus. There is only minimal evidence of an earth
goddess in Norse and Germanic mythology; Wagner's
prophetic Erda seems to owe her existence in the *Ring* to
the fact that Prometheus's mother was the earth goddess
Gaia, older than anything in the world except the original Chaos itself. Wagner probably got the idea of Erda
emerging waist-high from the earth from the many rep-
resentations of Gaia in Greek art that depict her thus.[18]

Later in the *Ring*, the cries of sympathy from the
Valkyries, when they hear of Brünnhilde's punishment,
seem to have been suggested by the cries of the Oceanids
at the punishment of Prometheus; the arrival of Waltraute on aerial horseback by the arrival of the Oceanids
in winged cars, the thunder effects in the Waltraute scene
and elsewhere in the *Ring* by the thunder and earth-
quake with which the *Prometheus* ends. Some of these
parallels, and those cited years before by Drews, may
seem at first far-fetched, but Schadewaldt is able to cite,
for most of them, verbal and even metrical echoes of
Droysen's German translation of Aeschylus in Wagner's
texts.[19]

Aeschylus seems to be everywhere in the *Ring*. At
least, Schadewaldt thought so. On the other hand, L.J.
Rather, the late Stanford professor of medicine, says in
his book on the *Ring* that if you really want to understand Wagner's cycle you will read Sophocles' *Oedipus*[20]

– and to detail that would take another book the size of this one.

Finally on the *Ring*: most of it is built up of scenes in which only two or, rarely, three characters speak. It is almost as if Wagner were limited, as Aeschylus was, to two or, rarely, three actors. And those long duologues – between Wotan and Fricka, Siegmund and Brünnhilde, Brünnhilde and Wotan, Wotan and Mime, Wotan and Alberich, Wotan and Siegfried – are all *agones*, protracted clashes of wills, as so often in Greek drama. But surely the most significant of the Aeschylean methods developed by Wagner in the *Ring* is the one we already noted in discussing the *Oresteia* – his use of leitmotifs. Wagner had used recurrent musical themes in all of his previous operas. It was a technique he had learned from Weber and other predecessors. But to use them so that they took on additional meanings, associations, and even identifications as they recurred singly and in combination – this was something he found in the shifting, multivalent, endlessly suggestive images in Aeschylus's *Oresteia* as nowhere else in the literature he read.

All of these suggestions that Greek drama shaped the structure, the events, and even the musical nature of the *Ring* are supported by the repeated observation made in the diaries of his second wife, Cosima, the daughter of Franz Liszt, that Wagner wrote his music in the morning and read Aeschylus and Sophocles in the afternoon.

IV

Wagner interrupted the composition of the *Ring* to write *Tristan und Isolde* – another work that may not seem on the surface very Greek. But it is, this long and eventful story compressed into three acts in which virtually nothing happens for long half-hours except in the orchestra. *Tristan* is, from a structural point of view, in fact the most Aeschylean of all of Wagner's works. A half-century ago Professor Kitto memorably contrasted the way Shakespeare writes with the way Aeschylus writes, and took *Antony and Cleopatra* and *Agamemnon* as his examples.[21] Both plays are built from stories that are long, complex, and eventful. Shakespeare puts in practically everything he finds in his sources, including some scenes from Plutarch that aren't particularly germane to his theme but make for good theatre, so in they go. He starts at the beginning of his story and proceeds through the middle to the end, transforming it all with great poetry and insight, of course, but keeping his plot a straightforward historical chronicle. Aeschylus, by contrast, tears his even longer and more complicated story to bits, selects a starting point somewhere near the end, and proceeds onwards from there. Those bits of the story he doesn't need – the ten-year history of the Trojan War, the death of Hector at the hands of Achilles, the Trojan horse – he simply discards. The bits he decides to use he doesn't use in simple chronological order but in the order that suits his dramatic purposes. He builds outwards from an idea.

Now listen to Wagner, in his prose work *Music of the Future*, on how he wrote the text of *Tristan und Isolde*:

> I plunged with confidence into what transpires in the depths of the human soul, and from that centre ... I dared to reconstruct the story's outer form. That explains why

my actual text is so brief ... I presumed to turn my attention solely to the exposition of inner reality and not to outer concerns of plot (which a poet dealing with historical material would have to occupy himself with). [In *Tristan*] everything that happens in the outer world depends solely on the inner working of the souls [of the two characters].[22]

To the casual operagoer, Wagner's music dramas appear, for those 'long half-hours,' to be static. But to anyone who knows Greek drama, Wagner's works, and *Tristan* in particular, are anything but static. Within Isolde in Act I and within Tristan in Act III, immense dramas are being played out. But they are inner dramas of passion, not external dramas of action. And that, by and large, is Greek.[23]

So overwhelming were those inner dramas of passion, and so superhuman the demands they made on the performers, that it was years before Wagner could get *Tristan und Isolde* on the stage. The Vienna premiere was cancelled after seventy-seven rehearsals, and when, after several more un-premieres, the work finally had its first performances, in Munich in 1865, the Tristan, still in his twenties and a giant of a man, died of his exertions. His wife, who sang Isolde, retreated into spiritualism, half mad. An assistant conductor actually did go mad during rehearsals. The chief conductor, Hans von Bülow, wrote, 'My intensive work on *Tristan*, that gigantic and devastating score, has literally finished me.' His wife Cosima left him – for Richard Wagner. Wagner himself managed, in the midst of this, to secure a political pardon, return to his homeland, lose his now unsympathetic first wife, confound his critics, and find new patrons, not least of them the young King Ludwig II of Bavaria. Artistically, he was ready for something quite different from the 'immense dramas of inner passion' that raged in *Tristan und Isolde*.

V

Wagner turned to a project that he had first considered some fifteen years before – *Die Meistersinger von Nürnberg*, the longest of his major works, and the only comedy among them. It doesn't seem at first to be Greek at all. But it is, this song-filled vision of what people in an unspoiled society are really like – charming, lively, productive, and above all interested in art and instinctively right in their response to it. Years before, that was Wagner's idealized picture of Greece, and in *Die Meistersinger* it is his idealized picture of what the German *Volk* had it in them to become, if they would listen and learn from their philosophical shoemaker poet, Hans Sachs – that is to say, from their own German artistic and cultural traditions. Sachs tells his people, after a Midsummer's Eve when irrational Poltergeister were on the loose, that if they respect their own traditions they will conjure up 'gute Geister,' good spirits. Can that mean, *mutatis mutandis*, that with respect for their traditions they can turn irrational Furies to kindly Eumenides? I don't suppose anyone would have guessed that Hans Sachs's final address to the crowd in *Die Meistersinger* was inspired by Athena's persuasive scene at the end of the *Eumenides* but, wonder of wonders, we have Wagner's own word that it was.[24]

Schadewaldt has, predictably, seen even more of Greece in Wagner's comedy. At first one is tempted to dismiss as fanciful his suggestion that there is a correlation between the character of Hans Sachs and that of Plato's Socrates. The Nuremberg of Sachs seems altogether too far removed in time and spirit from the Athens of Socrates for any such comparison. But eventually one listens to Herr Schadewaldt. Both Socrates and Sachs are wily strategists in their educational methods. (Schadewaldt refers deliciously to 'das Kobaldartige, das Bösartige, das Schabernacktreiben, das Katz- und Mausspeilen' in Sachs – his mischievous hobgoblin-manoeuvring, his almost malicious cat-and-mouse playing with Beckmesser.) And yet each man, when we see within his soul – and we certainly see into Sachs's soul in the prelude to Act III of his opera – possesses a wonderful inner beauty ('Gotterbilder in seinem Innern'). This is a reference to Plato's *Symposium*, one of Wagner's favourite pieces of literature. We read there that Socrates is like the statuettes of the satyr Silenus on sale in the agora in Athens – outwardly ugly but, when opened up, veritable shrines, glowing with images of the gods.[25] Similarly, Sachs, outwardly not so young and handsome as Walther, is, within, the more beautiful man. Eva, the winsome heroine of the opera, as much as says so, though it is Walther she is in love with.

Schadewalt goes still further in the comparison: Plato's Socrates is childless, but acts as a 'midwife' to the births of beautiful ideas in others. Wagner's Hans Sachs is similarly 'kinderlos,' but helps with the delivery of Walther's Mastersong, and, when it is safely born, pronounces, 'Ein Kind war hier geboren.' The song, like a child, is carefully brought forth, tended to, and baptized. Of course Sachs is, in the context of the opera, a figure for his namesake, John the Baptist. But there is something of that maieutic educator, Socrates, about him as well. Eva too has learned from him, and exclaims, in a surge of simply wonderful music, 'O Sachs, my friend, what would I have been without your help? Through you I have learned how to think nobly, freely, intuitively. It was you that brought me to full flower.' Not even Socrates received such a tribute.

Is there anything of Homer in *Die Meistersinger*? On the surface, nothing at all. But for anyone who has read Homer and loves *Die Meistersinger*, practically everything. The opera's vivid sense of lives lived, the confident yet unassuming way it recreates a past era and all its varieties of thought and feeling – this, said Hugo von Hofmannsthal, the poet who provided the text for Richard Strauss's finest operas, 'is what we might call the "Homeric" element in *Die Meistersinger*, what makes it so solid, so fresh, so ever-young.'[26] And I would add, too, 'the generosity, the honest tears, the laughter, the wonder, the wonderfully intimate and touching insight into human nature,' and especially 'the delicious sense that everything we see means something more than we see without its ever having to be turned to a symbol.'[27] This last feature is quintessentially Homeric. Schadewaldt cites in Homer, as objects that are beautifully suggestive of meanings but not quite symbols, the clothes in which the body of Hector is to be burned, and the clothes princess

Nausicaa gives to the naked Odysseus. Similarly in Wagner the shoes, which are metaphors – but never symbols – for poems, metaphorically tell us more about Sachs, Eva, Walther, David, and Beckmesser than the characters themselves ever realize.

One of the extraordinary things about *Die Meistersinger* is how, more than in any of Wagner's other works, the images in the text fall into significant – and delightful – patterns. References to shoes, songbirds, and biblical figures ripple through the text, interact with the music and with themselves, grow in significance as they recur singly or in combination, and in the end finally constitute a whole aesthetic.[28] I would hesitate to call the effect Aeschylean (the images are too solidly rooted in the experience of seventeenth-century Nuremberg for that), but there is no question that, long before writing the text of *Die Meistersinger*, Wagner had seen how images could work this way when he read the *Oresteia*.

We have already noted that, when the idea of *Die Meistersinger* first came to Wagner, he conceived it as, of all the unlikely things, a satyr play – that is, as a short entertainment to be performed as a kind of pendant to three tragedies. Just as Aeschylus's trilogy about Agamemnon coming home from the Trojan War was followed by an amusing little satyr play about Agamemnon's brother coming home from the Trojan War, so at first Wagner thought that his three long acts of *Tannhaüser*, about a singing contest among the Minnesingers in the Wartburg, could be followed by a short and amusing piece about a singing contest among the Mastersingers of Nuremberg. As it turned out, the lilliputian satyr play Wagner projected became, as *Die Meistersinger von Nürn-*

berg, what the Guinness Book of Records calls the longest opera in the standard repertory. Wagner, when he returned to his original idea in the fullness of his powers, saw in the little situation, the song contest, a unique opportunity to create a work of art about the creation of a work of art, and to prove that comedy could deal as profoundly as tragedy with human experience.

While we are talking about comedy, we should mention the foremost name in ancient Greek comedy – Aristophanes. Wagner read him a lot, and reading him was not without its unfortunate result. Aristophanes wrote brilliant and imaginative but rather nasty comedies during the war between Athens and Sparta. During the war between France and Germany, the Franco-Prussian War, Wagner tried his hand at writing the text of a comedy in the style of Aristophanes. He called it *Eine Kapitulation* (*A Surrender*) and subtitled it 'A Comedy by Aristop Hanes.' It was neither brilliant nor imaginative, only nasty. And it lost him many friends in France. Wagner was amazed that people didn't get the point: when he made fun of France starved out and surrendering to Germany, he thought he was showing, *à la* Aristophanes, that France had lost the war but won the peace: the play ends with French operetta triumphant over German opera. Those who were not amused, he thought, didn't know their Aristophanes. No one was amused. He had miscalculated badly. It wasn't, of course, the only time he did so.

VI

In 1869 an impressive and impressionable young professor of Greek entered Wagner's life. On Pentecost Sunday,

Friedrich Nietzche walked around the Lake of Lucerne to Tribschen, a house picturesquely set under Mount Pilatus, where Wagner was waiting out another Swiss exile. He had been driven out of Munich by his creditors, by Ludwig II's counsellors, who were outraged when he started to tell the king how to run the government, and by the scandal he provoked when he began his relationship with Cosima and lied to the king about it.

Nietzsche stood outside the house for a long time, listening as he heard from within a chord struck over and over on the piano. Wagner was writing *Siegfried*. Eventually the twenty-five-year-old classical philologist struck up his courage, introduced himself, and thereafter spent many long days and nights in conversation with the composer now at the height of his powers. Awarded his doctorate at nineteen without having written a dissertation but solely on his colleagues's recommendation for a professor's chair at the University of Basel, young Nietzsche was as eager to sit at the feet of genius as the scholarly world was eager to put Nietzsche's first publication to the test.

Wagner was overjoyed to have found a promising young intellectual who admired his work. He hoped that he and Nietzsche, the poet and the thinker (Wagner called the two of them Homer and Plato) would effect together a great Renaissance, and that Homer, filled with the ideas of Plato, would become 'the greatest Homer of all.'[29] Cosima was wary, even though Nietzsche was content to run errands and help trim the Christmas tree. Nietzsche thought he had found in Wagner, not Homer, but Aeschylus come alive again. Unwisely, he said as much in print. It was not the sort of thing his fellow academics expected of a Herr Professor Doctor.

Nietzsche's first book, *The Birth of Tragedy from the Spirit of Music*, was dedicated to Wagner. Its main insight – that Greek drama, indeed the whole phenomenon of ancient Greek civilization, was a synthesis of Apollo and Dionysus, of the rational and the irrational – was an idea that was startlingly new then and is still yielding increase today. But *The Birth of Tragedy* was as frenzied, if not quite as foggy, as Wagner's first prose works had been. It was a brilliant argument unsupported by the required scholarly apparatus. And by the closing chapters it had turned into little more than propaganda for what the opposition thought the 'supposedly' important work of one Richard Wagner. Another young professor, one who was to become a great classicist – Ulrich von Wilamowitz-Moellendorf – led the forces of opposition, gleefully scornful. The real professors wanted the dilettantes out of the groves of academe. They wanted Nietzsche's head. His students turned on him, and that, at a German university, spelled disaster. Nietzsche gave up his promising academic career. It was traumatic for him, but it set him on an even greater course. He turned to philosophy, pioneered much of twentieth-century thought, and many of his ideas are only now coming into their own. Philology's loss was philosophy's gain.

How much does *The Birth of Tragedy* owe to Wagner? It is one of the major disappointments of Cosima's diaries that she doesn't fill us in on the answers. We read that Wagner and Nietzsche had long, interesting conversations about Greek drama, that Nietzsche sometimes brought along on his visits to Tribschen another young classicist, soon to be famous as well – Erwin Rohde. But we can't say much more than that Wagner provided the initial inspiration for the book, that Wagner and Cosima were not happy with the first drafts, and that Nietzsche added more – the last two chapters, where he says that his new ideas on Greek tragedy have already been realized in the operas of Richard Wagner. The controversy did not abate when Wagner wrote an 'Open Letter to Friedrich Nietzsche' in the *Norddeutscher Allgemeine Zeitung*, encouraging his protégé and pouring scorn, not just on Wilamowitz, but on philologists in general. Then he moved to Bayreuth to build his theatre there, leaving Nietzsche's defence to Erwin Rohde.

When Nietzsche turned to philosophy, Wagner was in part the model for his superman. But not even Wagner could live up to Nietzsche's superhuman ideals. The Dionysiac fever in Wagner's music was Nietzsche's delight and despair all his life. But the Wagnerian ideas in the last chapters of *The Birth of Tragedy* he later repudiated. He began to see Wagner as an actor, not an artist, as a self-dramatizing personality who would tolerate no other personality as dramatic as himself. Wagner, characteristically, started to tell Nietzsche how to run his life.

Nietzsche broke with Wagner completely over *Parsifal*. In his last years the composer had turned to Christian myth and symbol, and Nietzsche thought, with some justification, that his erstwhile idol had capitulated to bourgeois Christian piety, not because he believed, but because he had to curry favour with Europe's moneyed classes in order to finance his crowning project, the theatre at Bayreuth. Nietzsche was sickened that his Aeschylus *redivivus*, the Homer to which he would be Plato, had, as he put it, sunk at the foot of the cross. He not only left Wagner, but hounded him thereafter in a series of scathing essays. They are still read, and not just as so much scandal. Though Nietzsche was already beginning to feel the effects of the madness that would destroy him, his anti-Wagner works are not mad. They are regarded now as containing valid and valuable insights into Wagner, provided they are read with proper attention to the storm and stress in them. That is to say, they are right in saying that Wagner is essentially a man of the theatre, that his dramas are all attempts at self-understanding, that he represents Dionysus (the unconscious) as opposed to Apollo (consciousness). Today we recognize all of these things as Wagner's strengths, not his weaknesses. And they are strengths, by the way, that link him more closely to Aeschylus.

Meanwhile, Wagner, with efforts that would have broken seven lesser men, realized his dream of building that theatre of his own – Bayreuth, designed for and adequate to productions of his work, the theatre in which a new Germany was to be born, a Germany nourished, as Athens once was, by its myths. It has often been said that the Germany that Wagner rebuilt from his theatre came to fruition in the Third Reich. After the Allied victory over Nazi Germany, many people thought that the theatre ought never to be reopened. It may take another generation before Wagner – and Nietzsche too – can be reassessed with proper reference to the National Socialists who pre-empted and distorted their views.

Bayreuth was not the common expression of *das Volk* that Wagner hoped it would be. Its patrons were crowned heads, aristocrats, and moneyed classes. Wagner was disappointed in that. But in other important respects the theatre was and still is a marvel – a kind of Greek marvel, with perfect acoustics and perfect sight-lines, with no boxes or chandeliers but rather with seating democratically ranged in semicircular arcs and a darkened auditorium where the lighting on stage can be keyed to the stages of the drama, and with the *Ring* on the stage – a vast trilogy with a prologue, dramatizing for a people its own myths. Wagner had learned well from his Greek masters.

About the work specially written for that new stage, Wagner's final opera, *Parsifal*, it should be said here that the burning wound of Amfortas, healed only by the spear that inflicted it, is an idea not to be found in any of the medieval sources Wagner used. But it *can* be found in the Greek myth of Telephus – a subject once treated by all three of the great Greek tragedians. Their Telephus tragedies are now lost, but Wagner read of the myth in Goethe's *Tasso*.[30] Even in his last years, as success and recognition came to him at last, Wagner could still use an idea from Greece.

He spoke less and less of his Greeks near the end. He stopped reading Plato and came almost to dislike the violence in Homer's *Iliad*. He didn't need much of mythic or classic Greece to write *Parsifal*. In a sense it would have been a distraction in his Christian myth with a subtext of Buddhism. And too much Greece, too, would have brought Nietzsche to mind. He wanted that burning wound to heal.

And then, when his Germanic *Parsifal* was finished and he was in the Mediterranean world with only a few weeks left to live, Wagner was asked what in all of art he regarded as perfect, and he replied, 'an ancient Greek statue.'[31]

VII

What, then, do we say in conclusion? We say that Greece was a major influence on Wagner at pivotal points in his development, especially when, in exile from his German traditions and to an extent unsure of them, he needed a tradition to inspire him and a stimulus to start composing again. He knew he had music in him that was like no music ever heard before. To summon it forth, he had first to convince others and, more importantly, to convince himself that his ideas were somehow Greek, and therefore sound.

At the same time, we should admit that his best work was done when he had worked his way through his theories and could allow his musical powers to function unimpaired by and occasionally in contradiction to those theories.

So Greece is not everything in Wagner. It is not some sort of key to understanding Wagner. Greece is, however, a way of understanding yourself, and in that it is like Wagner. I would like to suggest in closing that, on some of the evenings to come, you take a leaf from Cosima's diaries.

On a typical evening at Tribschen Wagner and his wife ask, when the children are asleep, what book they should read together. Plato? Not yet bound. Schiller? Read him recently. Calderon? Shakespeare? Homer? 'We decide,' Cosima writes, 'on the last.' (I'm pleased at that, for Homer is far and away my favourite reading.) 'Most wonderful impression,' Cosima writes, 'a sublimely intimate evening, indelible images stamped on my mind. Untroubled sleep.'

In the next day's entry she writes, 'The evening [is] crowned with four cantos from the *Odyssey* (Calypso, Nausicäa, Leucothea). Only distraction during the reading is watching R[ichard]'s fine, radiant countenance and delighting in the sound of his voice.' And on successive evenings she writes, about subsequent books of the *Odyssey*, 'Great delight ... The splendid happenings seem like a dream picture to me ... [Richard's] voice and his manner encompass the immortal work like music.'[32]

One day, over lunch, Wagner rates Plato's *Symposium* above all other literary works: 'In Shakespeare we see Nature as it is, here we have the artistic awareness of the benefactor added; what would the world know about redeeming beauty without Plato?'[33]

One night they decide that there are seven great books. 'Over supper we discussed our indispensables and classified them thus: Homer, Aeschylus, Sophocles, Plato's *Symposium*, Cervantes' *Don Quixote*, the whole of Shakespeare, and Goethe's *Faust*.'[34]

The theatre at Bayreuth is opened, and they move into Wahnfried, the house Wagner designed there for himself. Properly married at last, they now have a library of over two thousand books to choose from for their evening reading. They make their way through several books of Thucydides together. Wagner wants to contrast German politics with those of classic Greece. 'Ah, they were too intelligent, those fellows,' he says of the Athenians. 'They could not last.'[35] One day Cosima finds him reading Sophocles' *Oedipus* and checking the translation against the original Greek. 'It is a torrent of beauty,' he says, 'now vanished forever: we are barbarians.'[36]

A son is born, and they draw up plans for his future reading. Philosophy: Schopenhauer. Religion: Eckhart, Tauler. Art: R. Wagner. And then, much the same great-books program as before, climaxing in the big three – Homer, Aeschylus, and Sophocles.[37]

There is something touching, finally, about the older, thoroughly domesticated couple, in an age before television, settling down again to read the *Odyssey* – she listening, as Penelope once did, and he reading the tale, as Odysseus once told it to his wife. He reads, she says, 'in so sublimely moving a way that I shed tears.'[38] He concludes that Homer 'really was the poet *par excellence*, the source of all poetic art, the true creator.'[39] (He's right, as usual, in aesthetic matters.) In his last year, they return to Book 10, to the magical description of Circe's island, and the appearance of Hermes there. When they lay the book aside, he says, 'How sublime it is.'[40]

I am a retired professor of Greek, privileged for almost

forty years to teach Homer, Aeschylus, and Sophocles in both Greek and English, and on several academic levels, and I sometimes wondered, in holy fear, if I'd ever be blessed with a little Wagner in my class. I haven't seen him yet, but, for the record, I should be able to spot him if he comes along. He'll be the tough-minded little Spartan with the impetuous Athenian air. He'll challenge my every statement about Aeschylus. And he'll race through three or four or more books of Homer while all the other boys are still puffing their way though the first. Or a least he'll *say* he did.

Totally impossible

NOTES

Chapter 1   Athena Sings

1 Goodman 1964, 13.
2 I have translated this and the following paragraphs from *Art and Revolution* from Wagner 1911–16, 9–12.
3 Schadewaldt 1970, 386–7 is especially careful to make this distinction.
4 See Wagner 1983, 342–3. *Mein Leben*, which covers the years from Wagner's birth till his fifty-first birthday (1813–64), was intended for private circulation only. It was finally published, with many excisions, in 1911. A critical edition based on the original manuscript was published in 1963. The best English translation, by Andrew Gray, appeared in 1983.
5 It is generally held that, while women participated in peripheral events during the Great Dionysia at Athens, they did not take part in the dramatic presentations, either as spectators or as performers. Half a century ago, Kitto (1951, 233–4) held that what evidence we had was 'clear and unanimous': women *were* admitted to theatrical performances, and all who thought otherwise (mainly high-minded Germans who exclaimed 'Ganz unmöglich!' at the notion of women attending comedies) were only following preconceived opinion. The Germans, however, have largely prevailed on the matter. No Greek theatre in fifth-century BC Athens could have accommodated both all adult male citizens, who were expected to be in attendance, and their wives and mistresses as well. But, as the plots of Greek tragedy are derived from myths several centuries older than the democracy at Athens, many impressive female characters appear in the plays themselves, most of them in rebellion against the established norms of society. (See

Pomeroy 1975, 59 and 97.) One of the reasons for the relative
unpopularity of Euripides was that he had his Medeas and Phae-
dras say to men assembled in the theatre what they did not want
to hear from their wives at home.

6 Passages in iambic trimeter, the metre closest to the rhythms of
human speech, were almost certainly spoken. Other common
metres – especially the iambic and trochaic tetrameters catalectic –
were rendered as speech-song. The more metrically complex choral odes (*stasima*) and what, operatically speaking, might be called
ensembles (*kommoi*) were fitted with melodies throughout. For a
discussion of how original these melodies might have been see
Pintacuda 1978, 35f. The choral odes and ensembles in Aeschylus
are much longer than are those in Sophocles and Euripides, but
with Euripides the music became more expressive – too expressive
to suit the tastes of Aristophanes and later fourth-century writers.
All the same, Aristophanes was quite willing to exploit in comedy
what he objected to in tragedy: Barker 1984, 113 describes, with
perhaps too much imagination, how the choral singing of the
frogs in Aristophanes' comedy of that name provides the rhythm
by which Dionysus, rowing across the river Styx, 'times his
stroke,' how 'the bubbles are treated as an instrumental accompaniment,' how 'Dionysus decides that the only way to slow the
pace is to take over the rowing himself,' how 'the frogs refuse to
abandon their prerogatives, and the passage develops in to a singing (or shouting) competition.' None of this would have been
possible with the use of regular metres and the limitations they
imposed. The passage was *sung*.

7 Plato in the *Laws* (7.812d) speaks of a *heterophonia* 'when the
strings sound one melody and the composer another' (on moral
grounds he cautions against its use in the education of youth), and
Aristotle in *Problems* 9.12 observes that in string accompaniment
'the lower string always takes the melody.' Whether such hetero-
phony – and the use of the lyre at all – were features of Aeschylean
tragedy is a question that is still open.

8 It hardly seems likely that the instrumental music of Aeschylus
was ever comparable in volume to that of our symphonic compos-

ers in the Western tradition. The sound of the *aulos* has been vari-
ously described as delicate (*teren*), plaintive (*threnodes*), shrieking
(*aiazon*), capable of producing many different sounds (*polyphonos*),
and even deep-thundering (*barybromos*). The instrument was
made of reed or brass (perhaps also of wood or ivory), was cylindrical in shape, with as many as fifteen holes, ending in a widened
bell (*bombyx*). Some *auloi* have survived, but we have neither the
mouthpieces nor the skill to bring them to life, and dramatic performances in Aeschylus's day may have employed as few as two
auletes, possibly only one. It should, however, be noted that a composition for solo *aulos*, awarded a prize at the Pythian games a
century earlier than Aeschylus, depicted Apollo slaying the
Python at Delphi. Though it may not have had a decibel rating as
high as Wagner's scene where Siegfried slays Fafner the dragon, it
was said to depict the Python's gnashing of teeth with frightening
realism (and may well be our earliest example of program music).
No ancient Greek stringed instruments have survived intact, and
while passages in Euripides (especially *Iphigeneia in Aulis* 1036ff.)
indicate that lyres and even percussion instruments were used in
his dramas there is no conclusive evidence of their ever being
used by Aeschylus. (In Aristophanes' *Frogs*, where Aeschylus
appears as a comic character in a competition with Euripides, he
explicitly rejects the lyre as inappropriate to drama.) But the music
of Greek tragedy may well have been more complex and, given
the phenomenal acoustics still observable in outdoor Greek theatres today, more imposing than this note implies. Surviving treatises on Greek music indicate a refinement of the single melodic
line (with the use of quarter tones and the possibility of rendering
melodies not only diatonically but chromatically and enharmonically) that is unparalleled in our music, and perhaps would be
beyond the comprehension of the most trained contemporary ear.
See Henderson 1966, 587.

9 Senta is utterly silent for two minutes after her initial scream at the
appearance of the Dutchman, and after a few words to her father,
remains silent for eight minutes more; Elisabeth does not answer
Wolfram when, learning that Tannhäuser is not among the pil-

grims returning from Rome, she silently begins her long walk
upward to the Wartburg to die; Elsa does not respond to King
Henry when he asks her to address the court; Brünnhilde says
nothing for several minutes when she wakes from her long sleep;
Kundry has only two words in Act III of *Parsifal*, though she is on
stage for most of the seventy-minute act. Wagner expected his
singers to act these wordless scenes expressively. Nor are all of
them given to heroines. Beckmesser has five minutes of miming to
do in the first scene in Act III of *Die Meistersinger*, and Parsifal
more than that when he reappears in the last act of his opera.

10 *Cosima Wagner's Diaries* (hereinafter *CWD*), entries for 11 October
and 27 November 1879.

11 *CWD*, entry for 23 June 1880.

12 *CWD*, entry for 24 June 1880.

13 *CWD*, Daniela's entry after 12 February 1883.

14 *CWD*, entry for 2 July 1869.

15 See Lee 1995, 86–91.

16 We are to presume that, in accordance with Greek dramatic con-
vention, some time has elapsed during the preceding choral ode.

17 *CWD*, entry for 18 November 1874.

18 Quoted in Westernhagen 1981, 560.

19 In contrast to the early tradition of limiting the number of actors to
two per scene, this is an instance of a third actor speaking, an
innovation of Sophocles that Aeschylus adapted in his later plays.
Typically, the third actor maintains a long silence before surprising
us by speaking or, in this case, bursting into song. The most
famous Aeschylean instance of this is the silence of Pylades in *The
Libation Bearers*: we presume he is a mute character until he speaks
his one pivotal response.

20 The trail of crimes that, for three generations, plagued the house of
Atreus (some of it only hinted at in Aeschylus's trilogy) is as follows: Thyestes, the brother of King Atreus, seduced Atreus's
wife; Atreus, in revenge, slew two of Thyestes' sons and fed him
with their flesh; Thyestes, in revenge, laid a curse on the house of
Atreus and slew him; Atreus's son Agamemnon, in revenge, slew
Thyestes; Agamemnon, not in revenge but to secure a fair wind

for his expedition against Troy, slew his own daughter Iphigeneia. The crimes continue in the *Oresteia*: Agamemnon's wife Clytemnestra, in revenge, slays Agamemnon; Agamemnon's son Orestes, and by implication his daughter Electra, in revenge, slay Clytemnestra and her lover Aegisthus. The Furies, embodiments of a primitive idea of justice, have in every instance risen from the blood of those slain and called for blood-for-blood vengeance. A new concept of justice must be found if the circle of recrimination is to be halted, and that is what Athena ultimately brings. It should be said that Droysen, in the translation that Wagner read, gave the curse of Thyestes on the house of Atreus more prominence than it has in the original. This may well have given Wagner the idea, very important for the *Ring*, of Alberich's initial curse and Brünnhilde's final undoing of it. See Ewans 1982, 29–32.

21 *CWD*, entry for 25 June 1880.

22 Dodds 1951, 40.

23 A case could be made for *every* tragedy that has come down to us from Athens changing the myth it dramatizes in order to make a political point pertinent to the year in which it was first performed. The earliest surviving play, *The Persians* of Aeschylus, deals not with myth but history – the still-remembered battle of Salamis. (It may reflect a period in which political themes were dramatized explicitly.) Subsequently, under the guise of myth, Sophocles' *Oedipus the King* may be thought to deal with the pain of the still-remembered plague at Athens, as well as with rising doubts about the veracity of the oracles issued at Delphi. His *Oedipus at Colonus* reaffirms his faith in Athens after its defeat by Sparta in the Peloponnesian War. Euripides' *Medea* concerns itself not just with its mythic story but with the unenviable status of women, resident aliens, and unorthodox thinkers in the Greek city state. His *Trojan Woman* depicts not just the destruction of Troy seven centuries earlier but the virtual annihilation visited by Athens on the island of Melos just a few months before the play's first performance.

24 When she is alone with her father Wotan in the second act of *Die Walküre*, Brünnhilde reminds him, 'Zu Wotans Willen sprichts du,

/ sagst du mir, was du willst; / wer bin ich, wär ich dein Wille nicht?' ('You are speaking to Wotan's will when you tell me what you will. Who am I if I am not your will?').

25 Ewans 1982, 244–5 suggests that Siegfried's Funeral March in the penultimate scene of the *Ring* – a peroration that many commentators find more heroic than the fallible hero deserves – may actually be a statement of the importance, in a man's life, of reconciling both 'male and female values.' Wagner told his wife Cosima that the Funeral March was in effect 'a Greek chorus, but a chorus which will be sung, so to speak, by the orchestra; after Siegfried's death, while the scene is being changed, the Siegmund theme will be played, as if the chorus were saying "This was his father"; then the sword motif; and finally his theme.' But Ewans adds that 'greater importance is given, both at the start and the finish of the scenic transformation, to the music of women ... Ultimately, honour must be paid to both parents. The verdict of the Athenians [at the end of the *Oresteia*] recognized this; and so does Wagner's funeral music.' (The quotation from Wagner comes from *CWD*, 29 September 1871.)

26 There is little doubt that the assassination of Ephialtes, who in 462 had reduced the powers of the Areopagus, figures in Aeschylus's play, though Ewans 1982, 31–2 feels that Droysen, in the translation and commentary Wagner read, stressed it 'with reckless anachronism, as if it were totally akin to the situation in contemporary Germany.' He adds that 'this one-sided reading appealed powerfully to Wagner in 1847 ... and corresponded exactly with the role which he hoped he himself could play when the German people attained unity, after the revolution which he then saw as imminent.'

Chapter 2   Intermission

1 Pöhlmann and West 2001, 8–9 think it more likely that the letters are not a melody but only 'an unsophisticated attempt to express the characteristic sound of the instrument in nonsense syllables,' a

kind of 'tantara.' The trumpeting Amazon appears in their volume as figure 1.

2 Pöhlmann 1970 and Pöhlmann and West 2001. All of the fragments that were known in the nineteenth century were transcribed into modern notation by Karl von Jan (Carolus Janus) in a Teubner volume that also included the then-known Greek treatises. See Jan 1962.

3 The stone was discovered in 1883, during the building of a railroad at Aidin near the ancient town of Tralles. W.M. Ramsay published the finding, without at first realizing that the small letters inscribed over the text actually made up the melody of a song. The letters were first transcribed into modern notation and published in 1891 by Carl Wessely. Beneath the song an elegiac couplet is inscribed; it seems to mean: 'I, this stone, am [here instead of] a likeness [of the one who lies buried]. Seikilos placed me here as a monument for the ages of a memory that will never die.' Possibly the stone commemorates the death of Seikilos's wife, and the 'memory that will never die' is his memory of her. The last line of the inscription (not of the melody) was obliterated when the stone became a pedestal for the flowerpots of the wife of the director of the railroad. Once thought to have been lost in the 1923 siege of Izmir, the stone was actually preserved by the Dutch consul there, and in 1966 it was purchased by the National Museum in Copenhagen, where it now rests. There are photographs of it inside the back cover of Neubecker 1977 and in Pöhlmann 2001, plate 2.

4 Winnington-Ingram 1980, 669 calls the tune 'diatonic.' This is encouraging to those of us who presume to sing it in public. It has often been observed that the tune bears more than a superficial resemblance to the modal melodies of Gregorian chant. Compare the Palm Sunday antiphon 'Hosanna filio David.'

5 See Heichelheim 1958. The music, known since 1918 as fragment C of the 'Berliner Notenpapyrus,' was inscribed in small letters over the words of a tragic chorus on the death of Ajax, and has been thought to date from the fifth century BC because, according to the practice of musicians of that period, the melody was not deter-

mined by the rise and fall of pitch accents of the text. Then, in 1952, two fragments from the remarkable papyrus find at Oxyrhynchus in Egypt preserved parts of text of a tragic chorus from Aeschylus's *Judgment of the Armour*, on the same theme. Heichelheim plausibly argued that the complicated metre of the Berlin musical fragment could 'be combined easily' with the complicated metres of Aeschylus's words from Oxyrhynchus. His attribution has, however, been questioned in Pöhlmann and West 2001, 58. Like the Seikilos stone, the Berlin papyrus disappeared for a time – with the fall of Berlin at the end of the Second World War.

6 See my discussion of the matter in Lee 1998, 5–7. Henderson 1957, 372–3 puts forward the view that the four hymns ascribed to Mesomedes, the only ancient Greek music known to the Florentine Camerata, are actually 'an erudite Byzantine reconstruction.'

Chapter 3   Brünnhilde Sings

1 Newman 1976, 1:45.

2 Wagner 1983, 35. It is possible, of course, that the 'Greek' *was* an effrontery.

3 Wagner 1883, 171. Lehrs, Wagner's young companion in Parisian poverty, was a German in Heine's Parisian following. He provided the composer with the article by C.T.L. Lucas that gave the composer his first information about the singing contest at the Wartburg and about the epic of Lohengrin. He also introduced Wagner to Ludwig Feuerbach's *Essence of Christianity*, the work that argued, famously, that God was actually a projection of man's inner nature, and strongly influenced Wagner's earliest prose works as well as the initial drafts of his Siegfried project. Thus Lehrs, who laboured unknown and almost without pay in the field of classics, may rightly be thought to have contributed to the genesis of *Tannhäuser*, *Lohengrin*, and the *Ring*.

4 When the debt-ridden Wagner had to flee Dresden after his participation in the uprising of 1849, the library was confiscated by the publishing firm of Brockhaus. They kept it together (Wagner's sister Luisa had married into the Brockhaus family) and eventually

presented it to the Wagner Foundation in Bayreuth. Among its over four hundred volumes are the works of fifteen classical authors in German translation and several works on Greek civilization. Of course later in his life Wagner built up a much larger library in Bayreuth. For details of both libraries see Rather 1990, 1–31.

5 One Eugen Mehler suggested that a melodic line in *Tannhäuser*, where the hero pleads with Venus for release from her pleasure grotto, could be fitted to the German translation of Odysseus's plea for release from Calypso's island in the *Odyssey*, and that here Wagner consciously or unconsciously reverted to the translation of the *Odyssey* he had done in his school days. See Newman 1976, 1:57–8.

6 Wagner 1983, 342. Droysen, the poet and historian of Hellenistic Greece (he invented the term 'Hellenistic') was still a university student advocating the unity of Germany when he translated the *Oresteia*, and his commentary interpreted the trilogy as a celebration of nationhood and a blueprint for historical progress. It is small wonder that Wagner was moved by it as a young man, but it is strange, given the debt he owed to Droysen, that the two never met. When both Droysen and Theodor Mommsen, the great Roman historian of the nineteenth century, were teaching in Berlin Wagner chose to visit Mommsen, with whom he was far from sympathetic, but apparently not Droysen, to whom he owed so much. See Roller 1992, 235–6, especially the footnotes.

7 Quoted in Westernhagen 1981, 100.

8 The paragraphs from *Art and Revolution* are translated from Wagner 1911–16, 3: 23–4 and 29.

9 Translated from Wagner 1911–16, 3:62.

10 Translated from Wagner 1911–16, 4:64–5.

11 Translated from Wagner 1911–16, 7:130.

12 The best summary of Wagner's salvaging material from his medieval sources for use in the *Ring* is Mertens 1992, 246–54. As for those who objected, as does the Penguin translator of the *Nibelungenlied*, that Wagner 'ultimately harmed the cause of medieval German poetry by inducing reckless distortions between us and

an ancient masterpiece,' Deryck Cooke answers, rightly, that 'the anonymous poet of the *Nibelungenlied* may himself be accused of intruding reckless distortions between us and several ancient masterpieces,' that both he and Wagner were 'taking the ancient myths and adapting them boldly (recklessly if one wants to use the word) to create a work of art for his own time.' See Cooke 1979, 83–5.

13 The first play of the Prometheus trilogy, *Prometheus Bound*, has come down to us in the surviving manuscripts of Aeschylus, but the weight of critical opinion today does not favour Aeschylean authorship for it: in language, style, and the needs of stagecraft it appears to be a work from the late fifth century BC. See Taplin 1977, 240 and 460–9. The two subsequent parts of the trilogy, *Prometheus Unbound* and *Prometheus the Bringer of Fire*, which depicted the reconciliation of Prometheus with Zeus and the establishment of ritual observances in his honour, have survived only in very fragmentary form. In Wagner's day, and in the Droysen translation of Aeschylus which he read, it was presumed that *Prometheus the Bringer of Fire* was the first play of the trilogy, and that it depicted Prometheus's theft of fire from heaven; hence Wagner's beginning the *Ring* with Alberich's theft of the gold from the depths of the Rhine. (A few commentators still hold the nineteenth-century view of the ordering of the three plays. See Ewans 1982, 256.)

14 Wagner wrote as many as six separate texts for Brünnhilde to sing at the end of the *Ring* before deciding he would let that 'new power' rising in the orchestra make the final statement. In the first two texts (1849, influenced by a naive hope that Europe's leaders would recognize the new values dawning in Europe) Wotan is left in control of a world redeemed by the death of Siegfried; in the third (1851?, influenced by Ludwig Feuerbach) Brünnhilde bids Wotan 'depart, powerless and free of guilt' from the world he built; in the fourth (1852, influenced by Bakunin and the Dresden uprising) Brunnhilde proclaims that 'the end of the gods now dawns,' sets a guilty Valhalla on fire, and hails the coming of 'a realm of freedom'; in the fifth (1856, influenced by Schopenhauer)

Brünnhilde recognizes that the world's course in meaningless and wills her own annihilation; in the sixth (1873, perhaps influenced by Hegel's idea of self-awareness) Brünnhilde says nothing about the meaninglessness of the world, there is a return to primeval nature, and the orchestra sounds across the water the musical theme that signals what I would call the Aeschylean emergence of a 'new power' to rule a redeemed world. For a matter-of-fact detailing of the changes in the text, see Newman 1976, 2:347–61. For an extended Jungian analysis, see Donington 1974, 262–73. For an authoritative last word, see Dahlhaus 1979, 92–104 and 139–41.

15 See Drews 1980, 18–20. Drews makes several other points as well. But he might have made two things clearer. There *is* a ring of fire in the sources – but it is only an obstacle preventing would-be suitors from access to an all-too-vigilant virago. And there *is* an old Norse earth goddess, Jörd, in the sources – but she plays no role in the stories. The fact remains that Erda is Wagner's invention, and so is Wotan's encircling the slumbering Brünnhilde in a ring of fire.

16 Some editors and translators treat the initial questions of these dreams as statements. But in Wagner's century they were thought to be questions, and punctuated as such. (Cf. the 1890 Leipzig edition of Paul Cauer.) In Homer the dream visions take a position at the head of the sleeper, while Wagner's stage directions have the dream-Alberich crouch before the sleeping Hagen, clasping his knees in the Homeric form of supplication. Most modern productions ignore Wagner's wishes and represent Alberich as standing, like the dream visions in Homer, over Hagen's head.

17 Late in the *Nibelungenlied* (Book 25) two water sprites warn Hagen that he and his Burgundians will be killed in Hungary. But, as Wagner chose to ignore the second half of the poem, the incident can hardly be thought something he salvaged for prominent use at the beginning of the *Ring*.

18 Schadewaldt 1970 2:361. See also above, note 15.

19 See especially Schadewaldt 1970 2:371–6.

20 Rather 1979, xviii.

21 Kitto 1951, 184–6.

22 Translated from Wagner 1911–16, 7:120.

23 Schadewaldt's suggestion (1970, 391–3) that there is a connection between Isolde's initial scene with her servant Brangäne and the scene between Phaedra and her nurse at the beginning of Euripides' *Hippolytus* is not convincing. Such scenes (compare Dido with her sister and Juliet with her nurse) are common in literature. And Euripides was of no interest to Wagner in his *Tristan* period.

24 See *Cosima Wagner's Diaries (CWD)*, entry for 25 June 1880. Lloyd-Jones 1976, 37 rightly remarks that 'the processes by which an artist's mind works upon the material which it makes use of are not always to be discovered by the light of reason.'

25 See Schadewaldt 1970, 397. The professor has won me over in the matter of Socrates / Hans Sachs, but his suggestion (393) that the contests in *Die Meistersinger* owe something to the contest between Aeschylus and Euripides in Aristophanes' *Frogs* strikes me as fanciful.

26 Quoted, in German, in Schadewaldt 1970, 2:398.

27 Lee 1997, 135, describing his feeling for Homer's *Odyssey*.

28 See Schadewaldt 1970, 2:399 and, for much more about patterns of imagery and metaphor in *Die Meistersinger*, Lee 2002, 117–26.

29 Quoted in Newman 1976, 4:261.

30 Schadewaldt (1970, 2:389–90) sees a connection between Wagner's young Parsifal sympathizing with the wounded Amfortas and Sophocles' young Neoptolemus sympathizing with the wounded Philoctetes. But of course the Parsifal/Amfortas relationship was already accessible to Wagner in his sources, Chrétien de Troyes and Wolfram von Eschenbach, and need not stem from any reading of Sophocles. Wagner did speak admiringly of Sophocles' *Philoctetes* in Cosima's dairies (see the entry for 16 April 1882), but this was not in connection with *Parsifal*.

31 *CWD*, entry for 23 January 1883. Wagner never visited Greece, and took little interest in antiquities or in archaeology. On a visit to London, Cosima (entry for 13 May 1877) identifies Heinrich Schliemann merely as 'the archaeologist' and describes him as 'not very impressive.' It seems that Wagner, also in London at the time, did not meet him at all. He remarked, late in life, 'If only a

few manuscripts of Aeschylus or Sophocles were dug up, instead of all the many statues' (*CWD*, entry for 13 April 1882). Perhaps when, in his last year, he referred to 'an ancient Greek statue' he was remembering with affection, like Rilke and many of us, the archaic Greek torsos in Munich's Glyptothek. He had lived for some years just a block away, on the Briennerstrasse.

32 *CWD*, entries for 2, 3, 4, and 5 January 1869.

33 *CWD*, entry for 9 April 1870. Wagner seems here to be classifying Shakespeare as *naiv* and Plato as *sentimentalisch*, in Schiller's terms. Shakespeare does not obtrude his own persona into his plays; Plato is self-aware in virtually everything he writes. This is not to say that one is greater than the other. We need them both.

34 *CWD*, entry for 13 January 1872. Wagner, sharing the opinion of many nineteenth-century Germans, remained unimpressed by Latin writers. Only Lucretius, Virgil, and Ovid are mentioned in Cosima's diaries. Virgil is a 'poet he cannot bear' (*CWD*, entry for 5 June 1882). The others are at best 'literature for the refined people in their villas.' Lucretius, Wagner thought, captivated his refined audience through erudition, and Ovid through wit, 'but that is all' (*CWD*, entry for 18 September 1870).

35 *CWD*, entry for 6 November 1871.

36 *CWD*, entry for 18 November 1874.

37 See *CWD*, entry for 16 August 1878. Others on the list: Darwin, Scott, Balzac, Machiavelli, Goethe, Schiller, Dante, Calderon, and Shakespeare. No German historians are allowed, though 'Greeks, Romans and English' are acceptable.

38 *CWD*, entry for 16 March 1879.

39 *CWD*, entry for 17 May 1879.

40 *CWD*, entry for 28 July 1881.

BIBLIOGRAPHY

This bibliography is a reference list of works consulted in the preparation of this study. It is in no way intended as a list of the most important works on Wagner or on classical Greece.

Arnott, Peter D. 1959. *An Introduction to the Greek Theatre*. London: Macmillan

Baldry, H.C. 1971. *The Greek Tragic Theatre*. London: Chatto and Windus

Barker, Andrew. 1984. *Greek Musical Writings I: The Musician and His Art*. Cambridge: Cambridge University Press

Cooke, Deryck. 1979. *I Saw the World End: A Study of Wagner's Ring*. London: Oxford University Press

Dahlhaus, Carl. 1979 [1971]. *Richard Wagner's Music Dramas*. Cambridge: Cambridge University Press

Dodds, E.R. 1968 [1951]. *The Greeks and the Irrational*. Berkeley: University of California Press

Donington, Robert. 1974 [1963]. *Wagner's 'Ring' and Its Symbols*. London: Faber and Faber

Drews, Arthur. 1980 [1933]. 'Richard Wagner and the Greeks.' *Wagner* NS 1: 17–21

Ewans, Michael. 1982. *Wagner and Aeschylus: The Ring and the Oresteia*. New York: Cambridge University Press

Fraenkel, Eduard. 1950. *Aeschylus, Agamemnon*. 3 volumes. Oxford: Clarendon Press

Goodman, Albert, and Evert Sprinchorn. 1964. Introduction to *Wagner on Music and Drama*. New York: Dutton

Heichelheim, F.M. 1958. 'A New Aeschylus Fragment?' *Symbolae Osloenses* 34: 15–18

Henderson, Isobel. 1957. 'Ancient Greek Music.' In *The New Oxford*

History of Music, vol. 1: 336–403. London: Oxford University Press

Jan, Karl von (Carolus Janus). 1962 [1899]. *Musici Scriptores Antiqui.* Leipzig: B.G. Teubner

Kitto, H.D.F. 1951. *The Greeks.* Harmondsworth: Penguin

Lang, Paul Henry. 1941. *Music in Western Civilization.* New York: Norton

Lattimore, Richmond. 1953 [1947]. *Aeschylus I Oresteia.* Chicago: University of Chicago Press

Lee, M. Owen. 1995 [1990]. *Wagner's Ring: Turning the Sky Round.* New York: Limelight Editions

– 1997. *The Olive-Tree Bed and Other Quests.* Toronto: University of Toronto Press

– 1998. *A Season of Opera: From Orpheus to Ariadne.* Toronto: University of Toronto Press

– 2002 [1995]. *First Intermissions.* New York: Limelight Editions

Lloyd-Jones, Hugh. 1976. 'Wagner and the Greeks.' *Times Literary Supplement,* 9 January 1976: 37–9. Reprinted in *Blood for the Ghosts: Classical Influences in the Nineteenth and Twentieth Centuries.* London: Duckworth, 1982. A condensed version appeared in Millington 1991, 158–61.

Mertens, Volker. 1992 [1986]. 'Wagner's Middle Ages.' In Ulrich Müller and Peter Wapnewsky, *Wagner Handbook,* 236–68. Translated by Stewart Spencer. Cambridge, Mass.: Harvard University Press

Michaelides, Solon. 1978. *The Music of Ancient Greece: An Encyclopaedia.* London: Faber and Faber

Millington, Barry. 1987 [1984]. *Wagner.* New York: Vintage Books

– 1991. *The Wagner Compendium.* New York: Schirmer Books

Müller, Ulrich. 1992 [1986]. 'Wagner and Antiquity.' In Ulrich Müller and Peter Wapnewsky, *Wagner Handbook,* 227–35. Translated by Stewart Spencer. Cambridge, Mass.: Harvard University Press

Neubecker, Annemarie Jeanette. 1977. *Altgriechische Musik.* Darmstadt: Wissenschaftliche Buchgesellschaft

Newman, Ernest. 1976 [1937–47]. *The Life of Richard Wagner.* 4 volumes. Cambridge: Cambridge University Press

Pickard-Cambridge, A.W. 1968 [1953]. *The Dramatic Festivals of Athens.* 2nd edition. Oxford: Clarendon Press

Pintacuda, Mario. 1978. *La Musica nella tragedia greca.* Cefalù: Lorenzo Misuraca

Pöhlmann, Egert. 1970. *Denkmäler altgriechischer Musik.* Nuremberg: Hans Carl Verlag

Pöhlmann, Egert, and Martin L. West. 2001. *Documents of Ancient Greek Music.* Oxford: Clarendon Press

Pomeroy, Sarah B. 1975. *Goddesses, Whores, Wives, and Slaves: Women in Classical Antiquity.* New York: Schroken Books

Rather, L.J. 1979. *The Dream of Self-Destruction: Wagner's Ring and the Modern World.* Baton Rouge: Louisiana State University Press

– 1990. *Reading Wagner: A Study in the History of Ideas.* Baton Rouge: Louisiana State University

Reinach, Théodore. 1926. *La Musique grecque.* Paris: Payot

Roller, Duane W. 1992. 'Richard Wagner and the Classics.' *Euphrosyne* NS 20: 231–52

Sachs, Curt. 1943. *The Rise of Music in the Ancient World.* New York: Norton

– 1955 [1948]. *Our Musical Heritage.* New York: Prentice Hall

Schadewaldt, Wolfgang. 1970. 'Richard Wagner und die Griechen.' In *Hellas und Hesperien,* vol. 2: 341–405. Zurich: Artemis Verlag

Schlesinger, Kathleen. 1939. *The Greek Aulos.* London: Methuen

Taplin, Oliver. 1977. *The Stagecraft of Aeschylus.* Oxford: Clarendon Press

Thomas, Glenda G. 1979. 'A Dialogue concerning the Music of Ancient Greece.' *The Classical Outlook* 57, no. 1: 1–4

Wagner, Cosima. 1978 and 1990. *Cosima Wagner's Diaries.* Translated by Geoffrey Skelton. 2 volumes. New York: Harcourt Brace Jovanovich

Wagner, Richard. 1911–16. *Sämtliche Schriften und Dichtungen (Volks-ausgabe).* 12 volumes. Leipzig: Breitkopf and Härtel

– 1983. *My Life.* Edited by Mary Whittall. Translated by Andrew Gray. Cambridge: Cambridge University Press

West, Martin L. 1992. *Ancient Greek Music.* Oxford: Clarendon Press

Westernhagen, Curt von. 1981 [1977]. *Wagner: A Biography.* Translated by Mary Whittall. Cambridge: Cambridge University Press

Winnington-Ingram, R.P. 1980. 'Greece I Ancient.' In *The New Grove Dictionary of Music and Musicians,* vol. 7: 659–72. London: Mac-Millan

INDEX

Aeschylus, ix, 10–53, 66–77, 79, 82, 86, 87, 90nn6–8, 92nn19, 20, 93n23, 94n26, 95n5, 98nn13, 14, 101n31; *Judgment of the Armour*, 50–2, 95n5; *Oresteia*, ix–x, 10–49, 54, 57, 66–9, 72, 74–5, 77, 93nn19, 20, 94nn25, 26; *Persians*, 46, 93n23; *Prometheus*, 9, 10, 47, 66–70, 98n13; *Proteus*, 43; *Seven Against Thebes*, 47; *Suppliants*, 47

Aristophanes, 34, 78, 90n6, 91n8, 100n25

Aristotle, 47, 90n7

Bakunin, Mikhail, 58, 98n14
Balzac, Honoré de, 101n37
Barker, Andrew, 90n6
Beethoven, Ludwig von, 62
Buddhism, 5, 84
Bülow, Hans von, 73
Bulwer-Lytton, Edward, 56
Butler, E.M., 58

Calderon, Pedro, 85, 101n37
Cauer, Paul, 99n16
Cervantes, Miguel de, 85
Chesterton, G.K., 11

Chrétien de Troyes, 100n30
Cooke, Deryk, 98n12

Dahlhaus, Carl, 99n14
Dante Alighieri, 101n37
Darwin, Charles, 101n37
Dodds, E.R., 38
Donington, Robert, 20, 99n14
Drews, Andrew, 67–8, 99n15
Droysen, J.G., 13, 26, 57, 67, 70, 93n20, 97n6, 98n13

Eckhart, Meister, 86
Eddas, The, 65
Ellis, Ashton, x
Euripides, 27, 29, 47, 51, 90nn5, 6, 91n8, 100n23, 25; *Helen*, 57; *Hippolytus*, 90n5, 100n23; *Iphigeneia at Aulis*, 51; *Medea*, 90n5, 93n23; *Orestes*, 51; *Trojan Women*, 93n23
Ewans, Michael, x, 93n20, 94nn25, 26, 98n13

Feuerbach, Ludwig, 5, 96n3, 98n14
Freud, Sigmund, 62

Galilei, Vincenzo, 52

Goethe, J.W. von, 10, 58, 62, 83, 85, 101n37
Goodman, Albert, 89n1
Gozzi, Carlo, 56

Hadrian, 52
Hegel, G.W., 99n14
Heichelheim, F.M., 50, 95n5
Heine, Heinrich, 96n3
Henderson, Isobel, 96n6
Hesiod, 30
Hofmannsthal, Hugo von, 76
Hölderlin, Friedrich, 10, 75
Homer, 11, 35, 55, 56, 58, 68–9, 76–7, 79, 82, 83, 85, 86, 87, 97n5, 99n16

Ibsen, Henrik, 19

Jan, Karl von, 95n2
Jefferson, Thomas, 54
Joukovsky, Paul, 33
Jung, C.J., 62, 99n14

Kitto, H.D.F., 72, 89n5, 99n21

Lattimore, Richmond, x, 17
Lee, M. Owen, 92n15, 95n6, 100nn27, 28
Lehrs, Samuel, 56, 96n3
Lessing, G.E., 10
'Life of Aeschylus,' 38
Liszt, Franz, 71
Lloyd-Jones, Hugh, ix, 100n23
Lucas, C.T.L., 96n3
Lucretius, 101n34

Ludwig II, 74, 79

Machiavelli, Niccolò, 101n37
Magee, Bryan, x
Mehler, Eugen, 97n5
Mei, Girolamo, 52
Merterns, Volker, 97n12
Mesomedes of Crete, 52, 95n6
Mommsen, Theodor, 97n6
Mozart, W.A., 62, 63

Napoleon II, 61
Neubecker, A.J., 95n3
Newman, Ernest, ix, 54, 96n1, 97n5, 99n14, 100n29
Nibelungenlied, The, 65–6, 97n12, 99n17
Nietzsche, Friedrich, 8, 78–84
Nordmann, J., 57

Ovid, 101n34

Peri, Jacopo, 52
Pericles, 16, 47
Pheidias, 47
Pintacuda, Mario, 90n6
Plato, 47, 75–6, 79, 82, 83, 85, 90n7, 101n33; Symposium, 75–7, 85
Plutarch, 47, 72
Pöhlmann, Egert, 94n1, 95nn2, 3, 96n5
Pomeroy, Sarah, 90n5

Racine, Jean, 62
Ragnarök, 67

Ramsay, W.M., 95n3
Rather, L.J., 70, 97n4, 99n20
Rilke, R.M., 101n31
Rohde, Erwin, 81
Roller, D.W., x, 97n6

Sappho, 47
Schadewaldt, Wolfgang, 68–70,
    75–7, 89n3, 99nn18, 19,
    100nn23, 25, 26, 28, 30
Schiller, Friedrich, 58, 85,
    101nn33, 37
Schliemann, Heinrich, 100n31
Schopenhauer, Arthur, 5, 86,
    98n14
Scott, Walter, 101n37
Shakespeare, William, 27, 55, 56,
    62, 72, 85, 100n23, 101nn33,
    37
Sillig, Julius, 74
'Skolion of Seikilos,' 48–50,
    95nn3, 4, 96n5
Socrates, 75–6
Sophocles, 27, 29, 47, 55, 85, 86,
    90n6, 92n19, 93n23, 100n30,
    31; Oedipus at Colonus, 90n23;
    Oedipus the King, 70, 86, 90n23;
    Philoctetes, 100n30
Stein, Heinrich von, 24
Strauss, Richard, 76

Taplin, Oliver, 98n13
Tauler, Johannes, 86
'Tecmessa's Lament,' 50–1, 95n5
Thidreks Saga, 87
Thucydides, 86

Verdi, Giuseppe, 8, 63
Virgil, 100n23, 101n34
Volsunga Saga, 65

Wagner, Adolf, 55
Wagner, Cosima, 23–4, 28, 25, 73,
    79–81, 84–8, 92n13, 94n25,
    100nn30, 31, 101n34
Wagner, Daniela, 24
Wagner, Luisa, 96n3
Wagner, Richard, ix–x, 4–50
    passim, 52, 54–101 passim
– OPERAS
    Feen, Die, 56; Fliegende Hollän-
    der, Der, 4, 23, 56, 91n9; Liebes-
    verbot, Das, 56; Lohengrin, 4,
    13, 23, 56, 57, 91n9, 96n3;
    Meistersinger, Die, 42, 43, 48,
    61, 74–8, 91n9, 100nn25, 28;
    Parsifal, 23, 54, 81–4, 91n9,
    100n30; Rienzi, 56; Ring des
    Nibelungen, Der, iv, 4, 16, 18,
    20, 23, 24, 27, 30, 31, 32, 34, 36,
    40, 58, 65–71, 79, 83, 91nn8, 9,
    93n20, 24, 94n25, 96n6, 97n12,
    98n14, 99nn15, 16, 17; Tann-
    häuser, 4, 23, 43, 91n9, 56, 77,
    91n9, 96n3, 97n5; Tristan und
    Isolde, 36, 64, 71–4, 100n23
– PROSE WORKS
    Art and Revolution, 5–9, 58–60,
    89n2, 97n8; Art-Work of the
    Future, The, 61; Communication
    to My Friends, A, 56–7; Con-
    cerning the Feminine, 42; Kapit-
    ulation, Eine, 78; Mein Leben,

13, 55, 89n4; *Music of the Future, The*, 63, 72–3; *Opera as Drama*, 61–2
Wagner, Wieland, 68,
Wesseley, Carl, 95n3
West, Martin L., 94n1, 95n2, 96n5
Westernhagen, Curt von, 92n18, 97n7

Wilamowitz, Ulrich, 80, 81
Wilson, Pearl C., ix
Winckelmann, J.J., 10
Winnington-Ingram, R.P., 95n4
Wolfram von Eschenbach, 100n30
Wolzogen, Hans von, 23